D1224415

The Rise

The Rise of the Skyscraper

of the Skyscraper

By

Carl W. Condit

 The University of Chicago Press

The University of Chicago Press, Chicago 37
Cambridge University Press, London, N.W. 1, England
W. J. Gage & Co., Limited, Toronto 2B, Canada

Published 1952. Composed and printed by The University of Chicago Press, *Chicago, Illinois, U.S.A.*

Foreword

THE architecture of the Chicago school today enjoys a worldwide recognition. It is no longer a "discovery." It needs no justification, no champion to win admirers. What it does need, however, is a thorough critical analysis of form in terms of the intention of the architects themselves, the structural techniques which they developed, and the subsequent evolution of architecture in Europe and the United States. Although many buildings of the school stand today, many have been demolished. Only two of the men who might be included in the school are alive at the present time. Scores of priceless negatives are decaying in the files of one or two commercial photographers. It is time that we discover what we can about this extremely important chapter in the artistic and technical progress of our age, before all that we know is forgotten in the growth of a large and dynamic city.

Americans have only lately developed a sense of their own cultural history. Even now they are singularly uninterested in the evolution of their most important activities—technology, industry, construction, and the building of cities. Source material for the historian in these areas is meager. Consequently, accurate data on the Chicago school are not easy to discover. The "Vasari of the Chicago school"—to borrow Sigfried Giedion's phrase—is *Industrial Chicago*, but it includes only work completed before 1891. This publication is a unique and monumental achievement, which should be duplicated for every major metropolitan area in the country. I have depended on it almost exclusively for information about buildings erected during the 1870's and 1880's. I have gained valuable insight and understanding from Walter Behrendt's *Modern Building*, Lewis Mumford's *The Brown Decades*, and Giedion's classic volume, *Space, Time and Architecture*. For dates of construction, names of architects, and technical details, I have made thorough use of a comprehensive directory of buildings in the Loop area compiled by Mr. Frank A. Randall, a structural engineer of the city. This work was subsequently published by the University of Illinois Press under the title *The History of the Development of Building Construction in Chicago*. For many buildings, however, I have had to go to files of old architectural periodicals in the Burnham Library, to the

Building Department and the Municipal Reference Library of City Hall, to building owners and managers, and to architects with long memories or good records. In the last case I am especially indebted to Mr. Elmer C. Jensen for his aid in securing information on William Le Baron Jenney and to Mr. Richard E. Schmidt for the material he provided me on the early work of his firm, Schmidt, Garden and Martin. For construction, design, and technical and architectonic details I have often worked directly in the field, the streets of the Loop and its immediate surroundings.

I must acknowledge two important debts in the preparation of this book. One is to Mrs. Dorothy Hofmeester, assistant in charge of the Burnham Library of the Art Institute. Only enthusiasm for the subject could account for the patience with which she provided me with all the information the library possesses on the Chicago school. The other is to the Committee on Research Funds at Northwestern University. It was by means of their generous grant that I was able to acquire the photographs essential to this publication.

Certain passages of this work were previously published in an article entitled "The Chicago School and the Modern Movement in Architecture," *Art in America*, January, 1948. I wish to thank Mrs. Jean Lipman, the editor, for her permission to reprint parts of this article.

CARL W. CONDIT

EVANSTON, ILLINOIS
April 1951

Contents

List of Illustrations

CHAPTER I

Architecture in the Nineteenth Century

THE FAILURE

THE word "style" is much abused. Yet its connotation is such that the critic and the historian of art can hardly avoid it. In architecture it represents or stands for those essential characteristics of construction, form, ornament, and detail which are common to all the important structures of any particular period in history. But it also stands for those technical and aesthetic qualities of the artistic product which grow directly, logically, and organically out of the conditions of human existence and out of the aspirations and powers of human beings. We rightly feel that the buildings of a certain style—if it is a genuine style—reflect in their form the realities of man's experience and the attempt to master and give emotional expression to those realities. These buildings are constituent facts of man's history, and their revelation is a part of truth itself.

The style of architecture which finally became dominant in the eighteenth century eventually faced the revolution in social existence produced by the birth of power techniques on a vast scale. The first clumsy steam engine might have seemed remote from the proud dignity of Lansdowne Crescent or Monticello, yet it symbolized a force that soon engulfed all the arts and all the modes of action of Western society. In the face of this unprecedented phenomenon the ancient and vital art of architecture suffered a tragic degeneration. And, equally bad from the utilitarian standpoint, the techniques of construction fell hopelessly short of meeting the needs and taking advantage of the opportunities presented by the age of power industrialism. We still suffer today from the medieval nature of the building art. The artistic failure of architecture in the nineteenth century can be stated very simply: It was the failure to form a style. It was the failure to provide, in its own vocabulary, an aesthetic discipline and an aesthetic expression of science, technology, mechanized industry, and modern urban life.

Architecture had once been what it ought to be—the *structural art*. It is the combined art and technique of designing, shaping, organizing, and decorating the stone, iron, wood, and glass of which a building is composed. It is not one of these activities alone; it is all of them together, making an organic unit with a form and expression and use of its own. But, as the nineteenth century progressed, the architect, instead of being a master-builder or a designer of a whole structure, became simply the person who applies a particular façade to a structure which had been largely designed and wholly built by others who cared little about the niceties of scale, proportion, and texture. This situation might have been tolerable if the architects had tried to develop an exterior form which grew out of and reflected and gave emotional expression to the dominant cultural factors of the time—science, technology, commerce, mechanized industry, and the new conditions of urban life in the great centers of trade and manufacture.

But, instead of trying to discover a mode of expression consonant with their time, the great majority of architects returned to the forms of the past. They lost all contact with the age in which they lived. Before the challenge of the machine they sought refuge in styles with literary and historical associations. They indiscriminately borrowed the exterior architectural details of one age and then another. Styles came and went like fashions in dress. In the United States the severe classicism of Jefferson and Benjamin Latrobe gave way to a Greek Revival, which was followed in turn by a Gothic Revival. Romanesque succeeded it, only to succumb to a newer passion for Renaissance and Baroque forms. With the exception of isolated structures and such extraordinary manifestations of creative originality as the Chicago school, this state of affairs persisted through the third decade of the twentieth century. It was finally and perfectly summed up in Le Corbusier's indictment, "We live in architectural zoos."

The eclecticism of the nineteenth and early twentieth century was not a product of ignorance or perversity on the part of the architects. Art is nourished by what a culture gives it. Architecture, in the period of its degeneracy, only reflected certain realities of existence in the industrial age. Its ephemeral, unstable, and superficial character revealed an inner confusion and disharmony which are in some ways even more pronounced today than at any time in the past century. In other ways, however, the split is being healed, and the world-wide movement of the new architecture is indicative of it. What the nineteenth century suffered from was a split personality, a "cultural schizophrenia," as Sigfried Giedion explained it. The emotional satisfactions and the aesthetic experiences of human beings were split off from their intellectual and practical activities. Science and technology parted company from art, and both were ultimately divided into an ever growing number of separate, isolated compartments. Eventually specialization reached such a point that one could not even see the world beyond one's own special activity, much less comprehend it.

Thus, at a time when the technical and intellectual elements of culture were most in need of human discipline, the one art best calculated to achieve it failed to recognize its very function. Architecture is a utilitarian art. Function, structure, and form are indissolubly wedded. Applied science and technology provide it with materials and with their known mechanical, thermal, and chemical properties; the artist's sense of form and order and harmony transforms them into emotionally satisfying objects that live in the imaginations of men while reflecting their ideals, aspirations, and capacities. A genuine architecture is a technical-aesthetic synthesis which makes it possible for the world of industrial technology to enter into the domain of feeling and morality.

In order to achieve this end, architects in the nineteenth century would have had to turn their backs on imitation of the past, for they were faced with conditions and opportunities which had no precedent. They had to master new materials and offer solutions to new problems. The forms of the past, however vital and impressive they once were, had little meaning for the conditions which came to exist in London or Paris, New York or Chicago. But there has never been a problem created by men which could not be solved by them. Although nineteenth-century architecture appears for the most part as a sterile desert of meaningless imitations, there were individuals who, consciously or unconsciously, accepted the challenge of their age and built directly and boldly on its basis.

THE CONSTITUENT FACTS

It was the engineers who first pointed the way which a new structural art would have to take. They built primarily for use, and whatever form their structures took at least had the merit of expressing directly, simply, and honestly the system of construction they employed. But some of the bridge engineers had a strong sense of form. They looked upon techniques somewhat as the artist looks on the materials of his painting or poetry, and they wanted to celebrate the powers they possessed by means of a genuine monumentalism. Industry had provided them with a new structural material, cast iron, and they exploited its possibilities with an exuberance unparalleled in the history of building. Early in the nineteenth century some of the bridge engineers, imbued with a sense of harmony and proportion characteristic of the best of the architects, developed a new aesthetic of construction that pointed clearly to an organic architecture appropriate to a mechanized industrial culture.

The first cast-iron structure was a small arch bridge over the river Severn at Coalbrookdale, England. It was built by the iron founder Abraham Darby in the years 1775–79. Following the precedent of over two thousand years of masonry bridge construction, Darby employed the deep arch as the only acceptable form. Thomas Telford's great project of 1801 for a bridge over the Thames at London involved a flattened arch of 600-foot span. In its size, its effortless grace, and in the delicacy of its iron ornament, it would have been an aesthetic achievement rivaling the best that the architects of the time could show. Telford's finest completed span was the suspension bridge over Menai Strait, built in 1819–26, the first important structure embodying a radically new system of construction.

The success of Telford's Menai Bridge led to the extensive employment of the suspension principle in Europe (where it had been invented), England, and America. Its triumph came with Brooklyn Bridge in the United States, built by John and Washington Roebling over the years from 1869 to 1883. Contemporary with this structure was James B. Eads's bridge over the Mississippi at St. Louis, built in 1868–74. For this bridge Eads returned to the older form, using a series of wrought-iron arches of 500-foot span. Equal in its architectonic excellence was Gustave Eiffel's Garabit Viaduct, completed in 1884. The great engineer of the Eiffel Tower first used the two-hinged arch on a large scale in the Garabit span and thus provided the structural art with another impressive form, the crescent-shaped arch truss. These immense bridges stand today, monumental pioneer demonstrations of a new and vital art in which the technology of the machine is disciplined to humane and aesthetic ends.

Nineteenth-century industrialization made repeated demands on the builder for structural forms which had no precedent behind them. The most important of these in many respects was the train shed of the large railway terminal. Again the engineer attacked the problem with his characteristic directness and courage and again succeeded in enriching the true art of building that the architect had all but forgotten. I. K. Brunel, in Paddington Station, London, 1855, created a huge vault of thin cast-iron ribs carrying a shell of glass and iron. The two materials were perfectly integrated in a form of great scale. W. L. Barlow's St. Pancras Station, 1866, and the first Grand Central Terminal in New York, 1871, revealed further refinements of the glass-and-iron vault. These train sheds embodied a prevision of the twentieth-century architect's handling of space not as an inclosed volume but as a free-flowing thing forming a part of a light and open structure.

Among buildings the most promising and original work of the nineteenth century was Joseph Paxton's Crystal Palace, erected for the London Exhibition of 1851. Paxton here reduced a building to a dematerialized, neutral skin of glass stretched over a delicate frame of iron members. The construction of the Crystal Palace was carried out by assembly on the site of prefabricated elements of wall and skeleton. It was an invention the useful consequences of which the building industry has yet to realize. As a matter of fact, the whole enormous significance of the Crystal Palace was largely lost on the nineteenth century. Architects neither appreciated it nor followed its precedent until after the first World War.

Paxton's work would not have been possible without the invention of cast-iron beams and columns to provide interior framing. This method of construction was used as early as 1800 in factories designed by Bolton and Watt in England. Its full possibilities began to be exploited when the American inventor James Bogardus in 1848 patented a structural system in which not only the interior of a building but even its walls were reduced to a framework of cast-iron columns and beams. An immense number of buildings in the United States were erected on Bogardus' principle during the next thirty years of the nineteenth century. The purest architectonic use of cast-iron framing up to the time of the Chicago school appeared in the Gantt Building in St. Louis, 1877. The façade of this structure consisted of an open pattern of large rectangles bounded by successive columns and beams and filled with glass. The Gantt Building clearly foreshadowed the impressive development of commercial architecture which came to be known in the next decade as "Chicago construction."

But revolutions in the basic forms of architecture occur not only as a result of structural innovations. They may grow out of very intangible things, perhaps simply an indefinable feeling about how a building ought to look if it truly reflects the dominant conditions and aspirations of life around it. The intuition of the artist leads him to see such conditions with unique clarity and to express them by means of the symbols of his art, whether literature, music, painting, or building. The formal approach to the structural art inevitably leads to one of the few architects of the mid-nineteenth century who understood the nature of the problems he had to deal with. He was Henry Hobson Richardson, one of whose buildings in Chicago we shall analyze at length. Richardson introduced no structural innovations. Except for the use of interior cast-iron columns and tie rods, he employed stone masonry as his building material. But in the vigor, daring, and imagination with which he molded the inert granite of his buildings he stood far above the rest of his contemporaries. He treated a building as a plastic thing, striving for a form and texture which would reflect the power and order of commerce and industry. Basically Romanesque, his buildings gradually took on a mature and original form which reached its highest excellence in the Marshall Field Wholesale Store in Chicago, 1885–87, and the John H. Pray Store in Boston, 1886. In that year Richardson died, just as the Chicago school was reaching its maturity. His influence on it was brief but profound and extensive.

THE CHICAGO SCHOOL

The architects who came together in Chicago following the Fire of 1871 represented the greatest flowering of creative talent that the history of architecture in the United States can show. Few of them were born or grew to manhood in Chicago. The city had no schools and only a handful of architects who could train apprentices. And, of these, even fewer were able to meet the seemingly impossible problem that faced them. To architects the Chicago Fire meant either a total catastrophe or an opportunity such as all history could not show. Among those who had lived in the city and those who had moved to it a kind of natural selection took place. Only the biggest spirits and the boldest imaginations remained to meet the challenge. Their success is attested today by scores of beautiful and useful buildings, representing the largest concentration of first-rate commercial architecture in the world.

The Chicago school is associated with the invention and mastery of steel framing and with the consequent development of the modern office building, hotel, and apartment block. But these categories hardly exhaust the areas in which the architects of the school worked. They embraced every type of building: residences, railway terminals and way stations, warehouses, factories, churches, schools, hospitals, museums, theaters, and even tombstones. Nor was their work confined to a single city. They designed buildings erected in New York, Buffalo, Cincinnati, St. Louis, New Orleans, Kansas City, Omaha, Milwaukee, Minneapolis, Pueblo, Salt Lake City, San Francisco, and Seattle. They were the acknowledged leaders of their profession wherever the dead traditions of the European schools had not corrupted American design. That they were either forgotten or condemned in the first thirty years of the twentieth century is one of the bitter ironies of our history.

Their achievement was not an accident, a sport produced in the evolution of Western architecture. They belonged in the main stream of a world movement. They were self-conscious artists and engineers who knew exactly what they were doing and why they ought to do it. They recognized their problem with a relentless clarity of insight, and the solutions they developed represented deliberate acts of intelligence and creative ingenuity. They were perfectly aware of the fact that they had created a new style of architecture, and for about fifteen years most of them never considered that any style drawn from the past could possibly fit the conditions they had to deal with. Many of them, most notably Root and Sullivan, wrote extensively about the technical and aesthetic factors of their art. Architectural journals and societies were founded in Chicago to record and preserve their words. The philosopher Sullivan, the most sensitive and subtle personality among them, recognized the real and lasting greatness of their achievement—that they had developed an aesthetic discipline of the powerful forces of nineteenth-century industrial techniques. The whole forward movement of contemporary architecture is in the direction of that synthesis.

The recorders of building progress in Chicago were also aware of the unique success of the local architects. The best evidence of this understanding lies in the pages of *Industrial Chicago*, whose anonymous authors were tireless in their praise of the originality and intrinsic greatness of "Chicago construction." They coined the phrase "commercial style" to designate a form of building which had no counterpart in the past. What is most remarkable, however, is their recognition of the union of science, technology, and art which reveals itself in the structural-utilitarian-aesthetic unity of the Chicago buildings.

Among the critics, historians, and scholars of the East only two men had the sophistication to see the importance of the architecture that was growing up in the rude city of the prairies. They were Montgomery Schuyler and Russell Sturgis. The latter consistently maintained throughout his life that the Chicago school represented the only genuine structural art of the time. He pointed out in numerous articles that no school of architecture could train men like Sullivan, Jenney, and Root, that it could not, as a matter of fact, turn out an architect at all, and that any real imagination and practical ability would be corrupted by it. He was right. The later passion for historical eclecticism, fostered and encouraged by the schools, ruined most of the Chicago talents.

A few Europeans understood and appreciated what was being done in Chicago, especially the French novelist Paul Bourget. But, aside from these and their few American contemporaries, the Chicago school had to be rediscovered in our own time. Perhaps the first to do it was Lewis Mumford, whose sensitive and discerning chapter on the school in *The Brown Decades* (1931) awakened interest on the part of those prepared to appreciate it. In 1932 the Museum of Modern Art in New York showed a small exhibit entitled "Early Modern Architecture in Chicago." A slim catalogue contained some new information on the architects and their works. Hugh Morrison, in connection with another exhibit of the Museum of Modern Art, wrote a comprehensive critical and biographical study of Sullivan published in 1935. The most thorough treatment of the school in its full historical setting appeared in Giedion's *Space, Time and Architecture*, published in 1941. Today recognition of the school is world wide. Architects, critics, and historians in Europe, North and South America, and the Orient know and admire the work of the Chicago architects in the brief renaissance that followed the disaster of 1871.

CHAPTER II

Chicago: 1871

CHICAGO had become by 1871 the focal point of commerce in the United States. Forty years earlier it was a collection of rude cabins on a swamp near the point where a sluggish stream flowed into Lake Michigan. By the end of the Civil War the expansive forces within it had reached an explosive pitch. The population had multiplied ten times in twenty years, from 29,963 in 1850 to 298,977 in 1870. The prairies of the Mississippi Valley had been opened to intensive agricultural exploitation. With agriculture came the institutions of finance and the facilities for the storage and milling of grain. The meat-packing industry followed the establishment of the grain exchange. The Union Stock Yards was founded in 1865 to centralize the processes of slaughter. The growth of operations at the mills and the stock yards was astronomical. It is no exaggeration to say that before another decade had passed the price of the world's bread was decided on the Chicago grain market.

Parallel with the development of agriculture was the growth of the railway network. The first line to operate in and out of the city was built in 1848. In 1871, twenty-three years later, Chicago was the hub of railroad systems embracing 10,750 miles of line, with aggregate annual revenues of $82,777,000. The carriers operated seventy-five passenger trains per day in and out of the city's terminals. With the railroads came the steel, coal, and lumber industries. From 1860 to 1871 the total shipments and receipts of lumber multiplied three and a third times, from 488,000,000 board-feet to 1,581,000,000 board-feet. In the same period total traffic in coal increased six and two-thirds times, from 151,000 tons to 998,000 tons. There were no blast furnaces in the city in 1860; there were four in 1871, with a total capacity of 160 tons of pig iron per day. The total value of manufactured iron and steel products increased five times, from $2,140,000 in 1860 to $10,467,000 in 1871.

But the bare statistics serve only as a mathematical measure of quantity. The dynamic quality of the city's life had no parallel. The fervor and devotion and energy that went into the production of industrial and agricultural wealth would have done credit to the most enthusiastic crusader. The discipline would have broken a martyr. The achievement was staggering, but so was the cost. Lewis Mumford characterized the Chicago of the early 1870's as "a brutal network of industrial necessities." Most of the dwellings were flimsy tenements or cabins. Railway tracks, yards, warehouses, factories, slaughterhouses, and dumps literally choked the city. The amenities of a civilized existence which justify the pursuit of power were largely absent. Yet the internal pressures knew no bounds once the riches of an undeveloped continent were opened to exploitation.

FIRE AND RECONSTRUCTION

The buildings of the city reflected the tempo of its life. Ninety per cent of them were of wood, particularly the houses, stockyard structures, warehouses, railway facilities, and the many barns that were uniformly scattered over the urban area. The commercial buildings of the central portion were largely of brick with wood floors and roofs supported by exposed cast-iron columns and, here and there, cast-iron beams. For the most part, however, where masonry was used, the interior bearing members consisted entirely of wood. Persistent wind, the carelessness of a people devoted to sheer practical action, and the absence of any safety precautions—these together with the physical substance of the city extended the most generous invitation to fire.

When it came, it struck with devastating fury. At nine o'clock on the night of October 8, 1871, a small blaze started in a barn on De Koven Street not far from Canal. The fire department, such as it was, had exhausted itself the day before fighting several fires which were traced to a planing mill near the intersection of Canal and Van Buren streets. The general area was a tinderbox. The Great Fire swept across the river and burned its way to the lake in a few hours. Northward it moved along Canal Street to the intersection of the north and south branches of the river, thence up the west bank of the North Branch. The old eastward-flowing portion of the river proved no barrier at all. The flames leaped over it and started to consume the north-side area. The fire finally burned itself out on open ground along a line which passed through the lower part of Lincoln Park. In about forty-eight hours the flames destroyed $192,000,000 worth of property out of a total property evaluation of $575,000,000. Approximately 100,000 people were rendered homeless.

The scene which one would have observed from a high point near Canal and De Koven streets was one of total destruction. Broken fragments of masonry walls stood up at infrequent intervals. Between them the ground was covered with blackened rubble. The so-called "fireproof construction" of the larger commercial and governmental buildings proved to be a tragic joke. In a heat of 3,000 degrees exposed cast-iron members melted into a completely fluid state. Molten iron set fire to whatever the flames could not reach. It was a dreadful lesson, but it had its effect.

Reconstruction began immediately and progressed with amazing rapidity for about eighteen months, but the panic of 1874 seriously retarded it. Genuine fireproof construction marked nearly every building which was erected in the burned area. In the first year following the Fire, 598 permanent buildings were erected. During the seven years from 1872 to 1879 a total of about 10,200 permits for construction were issued. The average was 1,275 per year, the low being 712 in 1874 and the high 2,698 in 1877. In the two decades following the Fire the total cost of new buildings erected in the city was $316,220,000. It was this vast program of reconstruction and expansion that gave the architects their immense opportunity and forced upon them the necessity of developing a new form and technique of building.

If we exclude the human loss, the Fire proved in one respect to be a blessing. Looking back over the new city that was growing out of the ashes of the old, the authors of *Industrial Chicago* could say, "Those fires were fortunate events for the Garden City as a whole, and none profited directly by them, so much as art and architects, for the flames swept away forever the greater number of monstrous libels on artistic house-building, while only destroying the few noble buildings, of which Old Chicago could boast."[1]

COMMERCIAL ARCHITECTURE OF THE 1870'S

The most obvious difference in appearance between the pre-Fire buildings and the newer structures which took their place was that of height. The radical difference in method of construction did not appear until 1885, the year the Home Insurance Building was completed. The widespread use of the elevator for commercial buildings made possible a sudden and marked increase in the number of stories, while the insatiable demands of commerce made it necessary. Together with the increase in height came a growing simplicity of formal treatment and a decreasing dependence on historical styles for the ornamental detail and form of the building. In few cases, however, did the architect abandon the precedents of the past. The materials of constructions were for the most part brick, cut stone, plain concrete, cast iron, small quantities of wrought iron, and wood. The best buildings revealed a simple dignity growing out of flat, unadorned wall surfaces and fairly large, uniformly spaced windows.

The commercial building with a sufficient number of floors to require the use of one or more elevators became common in the downtown area after 1875. The first elevator (steam driven) had been installed in the Farwell Building in 1864. Its newness together with its increasing numbers led to the designation "elevator building" for the new commercial structure. Its construction was uniform and simple. Interior cast-iron columns

1. *Industrial Chicago*, I, 115. (See Bibliography, pp. 249–50, for full entries.)

connected by cast-iron or wrought-iron floor beams supported most of the load of floors and roof. Column spacing was the same in both directions and relatively close, generally about 10 feet. There was nothing new involved in interior framing of iron. J. M. Van Osdel, the dean of Chicago architects before the Fire, was one of the first to use cast iron not only for columns but also for fronts, having employed them as early as 1856 in a block of five-story buildings on East Lake Street between State and Wabash.[2] Exterior walls of the elevator building were generally of solid masonry, brick or cut stone, strong enough to support themselves plus the floor and roof loads of the bays immediately adjacent to the walls. The foundations were usually pyramid footings of stone spread widely at the base and stepped up to receive column or wall. The building height was roughly proportioned to the speed and safety of the elevator.

The fact that the thickness of a masonry bearing wall increases in direct proportion to its height placed a sharp restriction on the over-all height of the building. The Chicago architects generally thought that at least a 12-inch wall was necessary for one story and that the base thickness had to be increased 4 inches for each additional story. Consequently, they felt that ten stories was the limit for a building with masonry bearing walls. The astonishing exception to this rule helps to prove the point. Burnham and Root's sixteen-story Monadnock Building, the highest masonry building ever constructed, rests on walls 72 inches thick at the base. The problems of adequate lighting and of utmost economy of construction eventually forced the architects to turn against the masonry structure once and for all in the case of commercial buildings.

The description of the typical elevator building which we have just given fits the great majority of large office blocks, stores, and multistory warehouses constructed during the 1870's and early 1880's. Among these were a number of structures which belong to the architecture of the Chicago school, and we shall discuss them at length in their appropriate places. With a few important exceptions, virtually all the buildings designed

2. The first structure with a cast-iron front as well as cast-iron interior framing was probably the Lloyd Block, built about 1855 on the northwest corner of Wells and Randolph streets.

by the leaders of the school were constructed in this way until Jenney invented the skeleton or iron framework in 1883. A typical example was Richardson's first building in Chicago, the office block of the American Express Company, erected in 1872. The total load was divided between masonry bearing walls and interior columns of cast iron. The exterior architectural treatment was Gothic, one of the few cases in which Richardson used this style.

The most important functional innovation to come after the Fire was a great forward step in the direction of complete fireproofing. The engineer George H. Johnson used the first hollow-tile floor construction in the Kendall Building, erected in 1872. The same material was shortly adopted for partitions and for covering exposed iron members. The result was that two of the greatest sources of danger in the event of fire were largely eliminated. The tile, being fire-resistant up to very high temperatures, remained intact in the heat of direct flames. The reduction in the amount of inflammable material in the floor brought about a consequent reduction in the total amount of material which could be consumed by fire. The tile covering of iron members was even more beneficial. The hollow space inclosed by the individual tiles acted as an insulator, and the iron could thus be prevented from melting and often from excessive buckling.

With the rapid progress in the technique of iron framing came many possibilities for even more radical changes in the design of a large many-storied building. The elevator made such a building practical from the standpoint of easy movement to upper floors. Fireproof construction made it safe. Within a few years the exploitation of these technical factors brought about the revolution in form and construction which became the basis of a fully modern architecture, emancipated from the last vestige of dependence on the past. But even before such a revolution occurred, and for a short time after it, the architects of the Chicago school were concerned with the technical and aesthetic problem of creating in masonry a form appropriate to the needs and the spirit of the new commercial and industrial culture.

CHAPTER III

New Forms in Traditional Materials

THE COMMERCIAL STYLE

MANY changes in the size, design, and construction of large urban buildings would have occurred whether the architects were capable of directing them or not. As we have seen, enormous pressures lay behind the whole building process. The architects had first of all to develop a new type of structure, the big office block of the crowded commercial area. The growing complexity of modern industry demanded concentrated administrative centers where large numbers of people could work at detailed and correlated tasks. The increasing centralization of the business process, along with other social factors, led to ever increasing intensity of land use. By 1880 in Chicago the price of land in the Loop district was $130,000 per quarter-acre. By 1890 it had risen to $900,000 per quarter-acre. Population growth continued to follow its logarithmic curve: in 1870 it was 298,977; in 1880, 505,185; in 1890, 1,099,850. The total urban area expanded nearly six times, from 35.15 square miles in 1870 to 178.05 square miles in 1890.

These conditions meant that the architect was no longer the free agent, molding the material of a building into a form expressive of his own spirit and feeling. He had a commission from society which he had to accept if he was to survive in his profession. The Chicago architects faced the challenge with unparalleled boldness, vigor, and imagination. They met all the utilitarian requirements of the great office building by introducing a bewildering number of innovations in structure and facilities.

They designed buildings to be erected in unbroken ranks along the city blocks. They developed structural devices and methods of construction that constantly increased the speed and efficiency of building.

The 1880's saw not only the creation of the iron frame and the curtain wall, with architectonic mastery of these technical factors. The period brought the first use of winter construction, which was adopted about 1881. By means of salt introduced into the mortar, bricklaying could be carried on in subfreezing temperatures. Through the insulation of concrete with straw and tarpaulin, pouring could be accomplished in near-freezing weather. A few years later the practice of using electric lights under temporary roofing over excavated areas made it possible for workers to complete foundations and basements in rain and snow. The next step was the employment of electric floodlights for night work. Only by methods such as these could the industry maintain the vast tide of building that came in the decade of the 1880's.

The architects never faltered. Technical ingenuity worked together with artistic expression. At first often unconsciously, later with full realization of what they were doing, they developed an aesthetic of functionalism which made possible the formal mastery of technical innovations as fast as they appeared. Yet they avoided a deadening monotony of profile and detail. They designed structures in quantity, story on story, block after block. As Giedion wrote: "Each [building] had its own individual appearance and its own name, and yet the aggregate appearance was not chaotic. . . . In the eighties the Loop . . . became the perfect illustration of American audacity in the direct assault that was made upon its problems. Whole streets were developed in a way that had never been seen before."[1] Correlation of form with a genuine style produced a new monumentalism.

With characteristic directness the authors of *Industrial Chicago* summed up the factors that determined what they called the "commercial style": "The requirements of commerce and the business principles of real estate owners called this style into

1. Sigfried Giedion, *Space, Time and Architecture*, pp. 291–92.

life. Light, space, air, and strength were demanded by such requirements and principles as the first objects and exterior ornamentation as the second."[2] One sees here the genesis of the simple functionalism and structuralism of modern architecture, of Mies van der Rohe's theory of "more through less."

Consciousness of what the architects were doing as well as enthusiasm for their work is revealed in the pages of *Industrial Chicago*. "Commercial architecture," its authors wrote, "is the just title to be applied to the great airy buildings of the present. They are truly American architecture in conception and utility. The style is a monument to the advance of Chicago in commerce and commercial greatness and to the prevailing penchant for casting out art where it interferes with the useful. It is a commanding style without being venerable. . . . The commercial style, if structurally ornamental, becomes architectural."[3] The last sentence is the most significant of all: it presents the basis of any aesthetic analysis of the work of the Chicago school and, indeed, of the whole modern movement in architecture.

The general architectural achievement of the city, together with the social and economic situation out of which it came, was admirably summed up nearly sixty years ago by a French visitor, Paul Bourget, in *Outre Mer*. "At one moment you have around you only 'buildings,' " he wrote. "They scale the sky with their eighteen, their twenty stories. The architect who has built them, or rather who has plotted them, has renounced colonnades, mouldings, classical embellishments. He has frankly accepted the condition imposed by the speculator; multiplying as many times as possible the value of the bit of ground at the base in multiplying the supposed offices. It is a problem capable of interesting only an engineer, one would suppose. Nothing of the kind. The simple force of need is such a principle of beauty, and these buildings so conspicuously manifest that need that in contemplating them you experience a singular emotion. The sketch appears here of a new kind of art, an art of democracy, made by the crowd and for the crowd, an art of science in which

2. *Industrial Chicago*, I, 168.

3. *Ibid.*, p. 70.

the certainty of natural laws gives to audacities in appearance the most unbridled the tranquility of geometrical figures."[4] The passage states, perhaps better than any other, the problems fixed for the architects of the commercial style and the accomplishment which they were able to make.

We have described the conditions out of which a new style grew and its general utilitarian and structural characteristics. The form which evolved organically out of these factors we may best understand by the analysis of specific buildings that represent what came to be designated in Chicago as the "commercial style."

PIONEERS OF A NEW ARCHITECTURE IN MASONRY

The new generation of architects after the Fire brought about a vigorous and progressive evolution of the commercial style before the invention and mastery of steel and iron framing. As a matter of fact, the high point of masonry architecture came six years after the first completely framed structure was built. The leaders in the establishment of a new architectural form were Jenney, Sullivan, Adler, Root, and Burnham. If it is possible to say that the new commercial style began with a particular building, the choice might reasonably be the Portland Block, constructed in 1872 at Dearborn and Washington streets, where it survived until its demolition in 1933. Its architect was William Le Baron Jenney, the most original talent of the Chicago school and at the same time the least conscious of the artistic importance of what he was doing.

WILLIAM LE BARON JENNEY

Jenney belonged to that type of American genius of which Roebling and Eads were leading representatives. A creative builder of the highest order, with a reckless disregard of precedent, he seems nevertheless to have possessed an objectivity or un-self-consciousness that made him largely unaware of his artistic achievement. As an engineer, however, he had that kind

4. Translated by Montgomery Schuyler and quoted in Schuyler, "Architecture in Chicago: Adler and Sullivan," Part I of "Great American Architects Series," No. 2, *Architectural Record*, December, 1895, p. 8.

1. CENTRAL MUSIC HALL, 1879 DANKMAR ADLER

Formerly at the southeast corner of Randolph and State streets; demolished in 1900. (*Commercial Photographic Co.*)

2. GARRICK THEATER BUILDING, 1891–92 — ADLER AND SULLIVAN
BORDEN BLOCK, 1879–80 — ADLER AND SULLIVAN

The Garrick Theater, formerly the Schiller Building, is at 64 West Randolph Street. The cornice of this building was replaced by a parapet in 1948. The Borden Block (*right*) was at the northwest corner of Randolph and Dearborn streets. It was demolished in 1910. (*Chicago Architectural Photographing Co.*)

3. 210 WEST MONROE STREET, 1881 ADLER AND SULLIVAN

This was originally the Rothschild Store (*center*). The seven-story building immediately adjacent to it on the right is Jenney's first Leiter Building (now the Morris). (*Kaufmann & Fabry.*)

4. JEWELERS BUILDING, 1881–82 — Adler and Sullivan

15–19 South Wabash Avenue (*center, with sign "Harmony Cafeteria"*). The building is now known only by its address. (*Kaufmann & Fabry.*)

5. REVELL BUILDING, 1881–83 ADLER AND SULLIVAN

Northeast corner of Wabash Avenue and Adams Street. The first two stories were remodeled in 1929. (*Commercial Photographic Co.*)

6. REVELL BUILDING, 1881–83 — ADLER AND SULLIVAN

Detail of the south elevation as it was originally constructed. (*Kaufmann & Fabry.*)

7. THIRD McVICKERS THEATER, 1885 — ADLER AND SULLIVAN

25 West Madison Street. It was demolished in 1922 to make way for the present movie theater. (*Commercial Photographic Co.*)

8. WIRT DEXTER BUILDING, 1887 — ADLER AND SULLIVAN

630 South Wabash Avenue. The original name is no longer used. (*Kaufmann & Fabry.*)

9. STANDARD CLUB, 1887–88 ADLER AND SULLIVAN

Formerly at the southwest corner of Michigan Avenue and Twenty-fourth Street; demolished in 1910. (*Chicago Architectural Photographing Co.*)

10. WALKER WAREHOUSE, 1888–89 ADLER AND SULLIVAN

The warehouse still stands at 210–14 South Market Street but is scheduled to be demolished for the extension of Wacker Drive. (*Commercial Photographic Co.*)

11. MONTAUK BUILDING, 1882 BURNHAM AND ROOT

Formerly at the northwest corner of Dearborn and Monroe streets, this influential structure was demolished in 1902. (*From Andreas, "History of Chicago."*)

12. DEXTER BUILDING, 1883 — BURNHAM AND ROOT, CLINTON J. WARREN

39 West Adams Street. (*Kaufmann & Fabry.*)

13. CHICAGO OPERA HOUSE, 1884–85 — Cobb and Frost

Formerly at the southwest corner of Clark and Washington streets; demolished in 1912. (*Commercial Photographic Co.*)

14. MARSHALL FIELD WHOLESALE STORE, 1885–87 H. H. RICHARDSON

Formerly on the block bounded by Adams, Wells, Quincy, and Franklin streets, this finest and most influential of Richardson's buildings was demolished in 1930 to make way for a parking lot. (*Chicago Architectural Photographing Co.*)

15. THE ROOKERY, 1885–86 BURNHAM AND ROOT

209 South La Salle Street. (*Commercial Photographic Co.*)

16. MONADNOCK BUILDING, 1889–91 BURNHAM AND ROOT

The original north half, at 53 West Jackson Boulevard, remains today the final triumph of traditional masonry construction. (*Commercial Photographic Co.*)

of supreme competence which made him perfectly confident of his ability. He lacked John Roebling's idealism, but he must have had something of the older man's almost lyrical exuberance. No one could do by accident what Jenney accomplished.

He was born at Fair Haven, Massachusetts, in 1832. He studied at Lawrence Scientific School for about two years and in 1853 enrolled as an engineering student at the École Centrale des Arts et Manufactures, Paris, from which he graduated in 1856. He got his early practical experience in war. He entered the Union Army in 1861 as assistant in the Engineering Department at Cairo. His rise was rapid. He became staff engineer to Grant at Corinth, shortly thereafter to Sherman at Memphis. The next step took him to the rank of chief engineer, Fifteenth Army Corps, Army of Tennessee. When the Civil War ended, he was engineer in charge, Engineer Headquarters, at Nashville. He was discharged in 1866, retaining the title of major, which he kept throughout his life.

Jenney came to Chicago in 1867 and established an architectural office the following year. Except for a brief appointment as professor of architecture at the University of Michigan in 1876, he remained at his Chicago office. The high level of his career, both in number and in excellence of his buildings, came in 1891, the year he formed the partnership of Jenney and Mundie. His appointment to the Commission of Architects for the World's Fair of 1893 seems to have corrupted him. He turned to the classicism which the Fair made popular, having designed its Horticultural Building, and from 1893 until his death in 1907 he did nothing that approaches the great achievements of the years 1883–91. In this melancholy respect, however, he kept company with many of the leading Chicago architects.

Jenney was not a narrow specialist. His learning in the history and science of his art brought him to the attention of editors and university administrators. His most important contribution outside the work of design and supervision was a series of lectures on the history of architecture delivered at the old Chicago University in 1883 and published in the *Inland Architect and Builder* during 1883 and 1884. The lectures included much new material on the results of contemporary archeological investigations into Hellenic and Babylonian architecture. He contributed several important technical papers to the *Inland Architect*. One of them, an expansion of a paper delivered at a meeting of the Chicago Academy of Sciences, dealt with the subject of the preservation of building stone. It showed an unusual amount of chemical and petrological learning.

As a personality Jenney impressed all who met him, but the impression varied extremely between that of the office and that of life after hours. The question whether he was an engineer or an architect has been debated since he first entered his profession. There is little doubt that he was both, but he was certainly not an architect in the accepted Richardsonian sense. In this respect we will reserve our discussion of Jenney's contribution for the sections dealing with the Home Insurance Building and later works.

Sullivan considered the matter in the amusing portrait of the Major which he presented in his autobiography. Sullivan regarded him as one of the few architects who "were intelligently conscientious in the interest of their clients," but beyond that the younger man was little disposed to hero worship. "The Major was a free-and-easy cultured gentleman," Sullivan continued, "but not an architect except by courtesy of terms. His true profession was that of engineer. . . . He spoke French with an accent so atrocious that it jarred Louis's teeth, while his English speech jerked about as though it had St. Vitus's dance. He was monstrously pop-eyed, with hanging mobile features, sensuous lips, and he disposed of matters easily in the manner of a war veteran who believed he knew what was what. Louis soon found out that the Major was not, really, in his heart, an engineer at all, but by nature, and in toto, a *bon vivant*, a gourmet. . . . The Major was effusive; a hale fellow well met, an officer of the Loyal Legion, a welcome guest anywhere, but by preference a host."[5]

Sullivan remained in the Major's office for six months. He was one of many Chicago architects who were trained by Jenney, the

5. Louis Sullivan, *The Autobiography of an Idea*, pp. 203–4.

most notable being, besides Sullivan, William Holabird, Martin Roche, D. H. Burnham, and R. H. Turnock. "William Le Baron Jenney," Giedion wrote, "played much the same role in the training of the younger generation of Chicago architects that Peter Behrens did in Germany around 1910, or Auguste Perret in France. He gave young architects the preparation they needed to tackle the new problems for which the schools could offer no solutions."[6]

The commercial style was plainly prefigured in Jenney's Portland Block. Except for interior columns of cast iron, the construction was masonry. The piers were of pressed brick separating relatively large windows. The building was five stories high, with flat walls unadorned except for narrow quoins at the corners and shallow rustication. The windows at the end bays of the façade were grouped into units of three; otherwise the openings were single and uniformly spaced over the whole wall area. A continuous projecting stone course above the first story and a small cornice provided a horizontal division that recalled the traditional base-shaft-capital treatment of the elevation which continued to disfigure many of Jenney's larger buildings. Full-centered or semicircular arch lintels formed the only interruption to the dominant rectangularity of the structure.

The Portland Block was a simple and straightforward design of geometric purity which took its form almost entirely from the requirements of a small office building. Every office had an outside exposure. There was little precedent for it other than the indigenous American predilection for plane walls with no projecting courses, lintels, or ornamental details. The Portland was popular as an office block, but hostility from the traditionalists prevented a duplication of its purity and honesty until 1879, when Jenney's first Leiter Building was constructed.

DANKMAR ADLER

Two buildings mark the inception of the architecture of the Chicago school as a distinct body of work. One was Dankmar

6. *Op. cit.*, p. 293.

Adler's Central Music Hall, completed in 1879; the other, Jenney's first Leiter Building, opened for occupancy the same year. Because of the unusual framing of the Leiter Building it is best to treat it in connection with skeletal construction. Adler's building, however, had the traditional masonry bearing walls. This forerunner of the Auditorium provided an early demonstration of the technical ingenuity which Adler revealed so magnificently in the later structure.

Eighteen years of engineering and architectural experience lay behind the design of the Central Music Hall. Adler had come to Chicago in 1861, at the age of seventeen, beginning his career in the office of Augustus Bauer. Adler was born in 1844 in Lengsfeld, Germany, which he left with his parents at the age of ten to move to Detroit. He had some elementary schooling there and at Ann Arbor, but he cut his education short to become an apprentice draftsman in the office of the Detroit architect E. Willard Smith.

The Civil War, as in the case of Jenney, interrupted Adler's career. He joined the Union Army as an engineer in 1862 and served in the Chattanooga and Atlanta campaigns. For the last six months of the conflict he was a member of the Topographical Engineer Corps in Tennessee.

Adler returned to Chicago in 1866 and entered the office of O. S. Kinney, with whose son he formed the partnership of Kinney and Adler in 1869. Their work consisted mostly of churches, schools, and courthouses. Commissions for office buildings came after the Fire, with the establishment of the firm of Burling and Adler in 1871. This partnership was dissolved in 1879. The Central Music Hall was Adler's first independent commission and his most important until 1881, when he joined Louis Sullivan in one of the country's most famous and most productive architectural offices. Adler was even less an architect than Jenney; consequently, the partnership with Sullivan gave him exactly the opportunity he needed to exploit his amazing technical virtuosity. While Sullivan concerned himself with the problems of planning and architectonic design,

Adler handled the matters of business and engineering. It was a perfect symbiosis.

The chief importance of the Central Music Hall is historical (Fig. 1). In it lay the genesis of the great Auditorium Building. It stood on the southeast corner of Randolph and State streets where it was opened for use late in 1879. It served its purpose for little more than twenty years, having been demolished in 1900. Adler showed no particular originality in the elevations and depended for the most part on a simplified Renaissance style for the treatment of walls, openings, and stonework details. The structure had a certain force and dignity, especially in the symmetry and regularity of the façade. The large number of openings, particularly at the base and the second story, pointed toward the open-wall construction that later became the distinguishing mark of the Chicago school.

The Central Music Hall was probably of masonry construction throughout, except for iron girders and columns in the theater. The exterior facing consisted of dressed Lemont stone. The columns flanking the entrance were of granite. The exterior treatment was chiefly disfigured by the pediments over the top-story windows, the row of corbels at the cornice, and that most persistent relic of tradition, the continuous courses at the top of the first, second, and fourth stories. This last element appears in otherwise fully emancipated buildings of the Chicago school.

The most distinguishing feature of the Central Music Hall was the perfectly functional arrangement of interior elements in what was then a unique kind of building. The Music Hall included in its six stories not only a theater but also a half-dozen stores and seventy offices. The stores were located at the base, the offices on the periphery of the theater, which was in the interior of the building. The acoustical properties of the theater were nationally famous and served to give Adler the reputation of the leading acoustical engineer of his time. This reputation justly became world wide with the completion of the Auditorium. The acoustical excellence of the Music Hall resulted from three characteristics: (1) the upward curve of the orchestra floor away from the stage; (2) transverse beams projected below the ceiling (the furring around the girders over the theater); and (3) the lateral curve of the ceiling vault.[7] Adler's mastery of acoustics appears to have been the product of a direct empirical approach to the problem. In 1885 he made a careful study of the Mormon Tabernacle in Salt Lake City as preparation for the design of the Auditorium.

Before construction of the Central Music Hall was completed, Louis Sullivan had entered Adler's office as a codesigner. The greatest number of important buildings in the evolution of a new architecture in masonry came from their firm. The presence of Sullivan's original and complex talent can be seen immediately in the work of the 1880's. The education and early training which helped to develop this talent were undoubtedly the richest and most varied that any Chicago architect enjoyed.

LOUIS SULLIVAN

The important facts of Sullivan's life are well known through his *Autobiography of an Idea* and Hugh Morrison's *Louis Sullivan, Prophet of Modern Architecture*. It is well, however, to recall the education of this defiant rebel, partly for the hostile reaction to schools which it produced.

Sullivan was born in Boston in 1856 of Irish and German-French parentage. According to his own account, he acquired the love of books about the age of twelve and the love of bridges and buildings a year or so later. Both enthusiasms remained throughout his life. He tells us that at the age of thirteen he learned that men designed bridges and that he then decided once and for all to be an architect.

Although his parents moved to Chicago in 1869, Louis remained in Boston, where he entered the English High School in 1870. He enrolled in the architectural department of Massachusetts Institute of Technology in 1872. He called the course there "architectural theology." It was mechanical, empty, and stu-

7. An analysis of the relationship between acoustical properties and the foregoing structural characteristics appears in the description of the Auditorium Building at the end of chapter iv.

pid, a succession of styles, orders, and details from historical handbooks. When we realize this condition, we can understand why some of the best architects of the Chicago school either studied engineering or had no higher education at all. Sullivan stood M.I.T. for one year, then left with the intention of studying at the École des Beaux-Arts.

Instead, however, he went to Philadelphia to live with his grandparents. Here, deciding to try his hand at architecture, he entered the firm of Furness and Hewitt as a draftsman. Sullivan chose Furness partly because of the superior quality of his buildings and partly because he heartily damned M.I.T. But the panic and consequent depression of 1873 ruined the architects' business, and Sullivan had to leave after a year at the drawing board. He went to Chicago in 1873. The city as he saw it was a mass of ashes, dirty ruins, dilapidated shacks, and scores of buildings half-finished amid the chaos. The crudeness and violence of the first immense efforts of reconstruction impressed Sullivan deeply. He loved the city and decided to stay.

His method of getting a job consisted of walking about the city, picking a building he liked, discovering the name of the architect, then requesting that he be taken on as a draftsman. By this process and an extraordinary intuition he landed in the office of William Le Baron Jenney. The building which had impressed him was the Portland Block. In Jenney's office he shortly found himself in the company of William Holabird, Martin Roche, and Daniel Burnham. It was at this time that he acquired his love of music, in good part through his close and affectionate friendship with John Edelman. The composer he most admired was, characteristically, Richard Wagner.

But the experience of the office was not enough for Sullivan. He went to Paris in 1874 and enrolled at the École des Beaux-Arts in that year. It was here that an obscure teacher of descriptive geometry, a M. Clopet, achieved some immortality by uttering a sentence that Sullivan made famous. Referring to the text in his course, Clopet once remarked to his student, "I suggest you place the book in the waste-basket; we shall have no need of it here; *for here our demonstrations shall be so broad as to admit of* NO EXCEPTION."[8] Sullivan afterward tossed all the textbooks in the wastebasket and devoted his life as an architect to a search for the rule that shall admit of no exceptions.

What the École des Beaux-Arts could offer Sullivan he had already learned at M.I.T. He found the French institution equally sterile and academic, carefully avoiding the acceptance of any real architectural problem. To study architecture as a series of styles seemed to Sullivan superficial and unrealistic, for it never penetrated to the heart of design and construction. He had to return to Chicago in 1876 to see the constituent facts in the structural art of his time. He realized then what every genuine architect of the nineteenth century had to learn—that most of the true structural art of his age was the work of engineers. They became Sullivan's heroes, along with the supermen Wagner and Michelangelo. His favorites were James B. Eads of St. Louis and Frederick Baumann of Chicago. The latter was an expert on foundations, and his book, *A Theory of Isolated Pier Foundations*, published in 1873, became the basis of many important innovations made by the Chicago architects.

Sullivan's interest in engineering developed rapidly into an enthusiasm for science. It centered mainly in biology, from which Sullivan's organic theory of architecture in part stemmed. He read Darwin, Huxley, Spencer, and Tyndall at great length. Thus his philosophy of architecture lay in the main stream of nineteenth-century thought on the subject, not only as it could be inferred from the new science, but as it was in some respects developed by Pugin, Ruskin, Morris, and Viollet-le-Duc.

Sullivan was often inconsistent, yet the philosophy which matured with his growing powers as an architect was original and profound. More than any other artist of his time, he understood the social basis, the responsibility, and the problem of art in a technical and industrial society. He felt that he had discovered the rule with no exceptions in the concept *form follows function*. The idea was first stated by Plato, but it remained for Sullivan to give it its systematic concrete demonstration in

8. Sullivan, *op. cit.*, p. 221.

terms of a contemporary building art.[9] The proper understanding of the word "function" is the key to his whole philosophy. An organic architecture, he believed, is one which grows naturally or organically out of the social and technical factors among which the architect lives and with which he must work. These factors embrace not only the technical and utilitarian problems of building but also the aspirations, ideals, and needs of human beings. Thus *functionalism* involved for him something much wider and deeper than utilitarian and structural considerations, as important as these are.

To Sullivan the creation of a genuine style was not a matter of historical styles or of dipping into a vocabulary of modern forms and details in order to secure a style which the architect might feel to be consonant with modern culture. The architect must first recognize the importance of aesthetic expression for the harmonization and emotional enrichment of the many practical and intellectual factors of contemporary civilization. In modern society such an art would start with the fundamentals, technology, industry, and science. It is the task of the architect, as Sullivan conceived it, to take the products of techniques, on the one hand, and the logic and order of techniques, on the other, and mold them into a form uniting both in a single aesthetic expression. An architecture so developed means the humanization through aesthetic statement of the nonhuman facts of industrial techniques.

The style of a building would become whatever the materials, structural problems, and utilitarian demands might make it. It would have to be partly determined by the ideals, aspirations, ambitions, and total human needs of the people who give the architect his commission. Thus a modern style would be a matter not of one form or another but rather of an organic shape taking form from the physical, intellectual, and emotional milieu in which it exists. Consciously or unconsciously, the architects of the Chicago school approached their task in this way, and their achievement must be measured against these criteria.

9. Socrates says, "The excellence or beauty or truth of every structure, animate or inanimate, and of every action of man, is relative to the use for which nature or the artist has intended them" (*Republic* x. 601C).

THE EARLY WORK OF ADLER AND SULLIVAN

After a series of minor positions Sullivan entered Adler's office in 1879, becoming a partner in 1880. The two men established the firm on an equal basis in 1881. The first building which Sullivan designed with Adler was the Borden Block, built in 1879–80 at the northwest corner of Randolph and Dearborn streets (Fig. 2). It was demolished in 1910 to make way for the present Woods Theater. The Borden showed a radical departure from previous masonry architecture. Except for Jenney's first Leiter Building, which is almost a framed structure, it was the first office block to break away from solid-wall construction.

In order to gain the maximum amount of light, the architects narrowed the piers and thus widened the bays. The strength of the pier was maintained by increasing its depth. Isolated stone foundations carried the piers and interior columns (the first use, so far as known, of this type of footing). Two large windows separated by a cast-iron mullion filled each bay. Except for the arbitrary horizontal divisions and the semicircular panels or lunettes surmounting the bays at the top story, the wall was a remarkably open pattern of relatively narrow piers and spandrels. The simple slab or cornice at the top provided an appropriate termination to the honest statement of function and construction.

The emancipation, clarity, and force which the Borden Block revealed were not duplicated by Sullivan for seven years. The Borden must have been the product of a sure intuition—there was no precedent for it in masonry building—but Sullivan's experimental temperament prevented his following its obvious truth. The next important commission of the firm, the building at 210 West Monroe Street (present number), showed a new departure (Fig. 3). This structure, completed in 1881, was formerly the Rothschild Store, but it has changed hands repeatedly since its construction. Here Sullivan first turned to the vertical emphasis, which culminated in his so-called "skyscraper" designs of the nineties.[10] Three continuous bearing piers of masonry

10. The persistence of dead ideas is remarkable in architecture. After seventy years the vertical accent still seems to be the inescapable cliché of skyscraper design. The office building of the United States Steel Company in Pittsburgh (under construction, 1950) reveals the same treatment.

carry the load of the Rothschild building, providing bays of 25-foot width. Except for the piers, the front is of cast-iron construction. The large glass area points to the mature work of the Chicago school, but the restless and exotic ornament, however original, obscures the essential form of the building and produces an effect of shallowness.

The former Jewelers Building, constructed in 1881–82 at 15–19 South Wabash Avenue, is free of the spiky ornament of the previous building, but the variety of openings and details in the façade betrays the absence of a clear goal in Sullivan's mind (Fig. 4). The over-all pattern of the main elevation, however, does reveal the construction: two brick piers close to the end walls divide the building into two narrow bays and one wide bay at the center. The original Revell Building, 1881–83, at the northeast corner of Wabash and Adams, shows progress in its greater regularity (Figs. 5 and 6). This building, still standing, was extensively modernized in 1929 through the application on the two lower stories of a smooth stone envelope surrounding casement windows set flush. The spacing of these windows betrays the fact that the bearing piers do not occur in pairs, as Sullivan has them in his street elevations. This is the first case of Sullivan's arbitrary treatment of the wall for aesthetic effect. The piers of the Revell are brick, the interior bearing members and mullions being of iron.

Progress toward greater openness and clarity is revealed by the Knisely Building, 1884, at 551 West Monroe Street, and the Ryerson Building, erected in the same year at 16–20 East Randolph. The latter structure was demolished for the present bus terminal at this location. The Knisely is unusually straight forward for Sullivan. Plain brick piers extend continuously from ground to roof. Solid masonry construction is presented as a simple fact, without adornment. Despite its exotic and vaguely derivative ornament, the Ryerson was important for the introduction of a great area of glass carried on an iron armature between masonry piers. The openings had the form of shallow bay windows.[11]

11. For illustrations of the Knisely and the Ryerson see Hugh Morrison, *Louis Sullivan*, Pl. 3, p. 323, and Pl. 6, p. 325. The negatives were apparently lost.

The steppingstone from the Central Music Hall to the Auditorium was the third McVickers Theater, completed in 1885 at 25 West Madison Street (Fig. 7). This old vaudeville house suffered an unhappy and baffling history. The original was built in 1857 and burned in the Great Fire. It was reconstructed in 1872, again in 1883, and remodeled in 1885. Fire destroyed the interior in 1890. Adler and Sullivan handled the rebuilding, which was completed in 1891. The new structure lasted until 1922, when it was finally demolished to make way for the present movie theater. It is impossible to determine exactly what changes Adler and Sullivan made in the exterior of the building. The ornamental lions' heads and the cornice are obviously relics of the 1872 or 1883 structure. Yet the unusually open wall, light and simple in construction and effect, is plainly their work. The building is a greatly refined example of the glass and cast-iron construction which represented the highest expression of the nineteenth-century structural art.

Like the Central Music Hall, the McVickers was a shell of offices surrounding the theater. The offices of the top story were added in 1890–91. They were carried on six steel trusses spanning the theater and supported by open trusswork columns carried on foundations independent of those of the walls. Many advancements were made in lighting, heating, and arrangement of mechanical facilities. Fireproofing, of course, was complete. The façade of the building is its important architectonic feature. It clearly foreshadows the great achievements of the next decade in steel construction.

The building originally known as the Wirt Dexter, with the present address of 630 South Wabash Avenue, was constructed in 1887. It is an even clearer revelation of the architectural expression of structure (Fig. 8). Sullivan eliminated the exotic and excessive ornament of earlier buildings, achieving simplicity while increasing dignity and force. For Sullivan it was the culmination of the old masonry architecture and close in feeling to the expression of iron or steel framing. Although the lack of uniformity of the façade weakens the general effect, the wide central bay and the narrow flanking bays in part make such a treatment necessary.

The influence of Richardson's Marshall Field Wholesale Store begins to manifest itself in the Standard Club, 1887–88, at the southwest corner of Michigan Avenue and Twenty-fourth Street (Fig. 9).[12] The Romanesque details, the rusticated limestone facing, the simplicity of wall treatment, the horizontal division of the elevations, the sense of mass together with a rich plastic effect—all reveal Sullivan's debt to the eastern architect. The interior showed the beginning of Sullivan's original and characteristic ornamentation. The Standard Club, demolished in 1910, was a fine work of architecture in its own right but even less in the main stream of Chicago development than the Marshall Field Wholesale Store.

A much more important work in the Richardsonian manner is the Walker Warehouse, 1888–89, at 210–14 South Market Street (Fig. 10). Like the Standard Club and the Marshall Field building, the Walker Warehouse represents the deliberate following of a certain form of masonry architecture rather than a logical step in the development of the commercial style. It is interesting, however, as an assimilation of the Richardsonian form in a way which points more clearly in the new direction. It is a solid geometric mass, with no rustication to interrupt its sharp-edged rectangular profile or its smooth planes. The arches and the various openings are firmly and positively integrated. For all its intrinsic excellence, however, it stands at a great distance from Sullivan's later work, which shows so skilful a mastery of the new structural techniques.

The Auditorium was the triumph in the traditional materials of construction. But, because of its complexity and the multitude of paths it opened to the structural art, it must be treated at length in a separate section. Moreover, the careers and early achievements of Burnham and Root largely parallel those of Adler and Sullivan and consequently require our consideration.[13]

12. On Richardson's building see chapter iii, the section on "The Marshall Field Wholesale Store."

13. Adler and Sullivan enjoyed many more commissions than those I have discussed here. The most important for the evolution of the Chicago school are the following: Rosenfeld Building, 1881–82, Washington and Halsted streets; Brunswick and Balke factory and warehouse, 1881–83, Orleans, Huron, Sedgwick, and Superior streets; Hammond Library (now Union Theological College), 1882, 44 North Ashland Boulevard; Frankenthal Building, 1882, 141 South Wells Street (de-

DANIEL BURNHAM

If Daniel Hudson Burnham had lived anywhere except in the city of Chicago, he would not have been the architect that he was. Frank Lloyd Wright has always referred to him as an "impresario," and there is little doubt that Sullivan felt the same way. The great designs that came from the office of Burnham and Root were the work of the latter. After Root's death in 1891, as long as fine architecture flourished in Chicago, the work of Burnham's office continued at a high level. As soon as the poison of the World's Fair began to work, however, Burnham succumbed. He enjoyed the greatest success of the Chicago architects, but he paid the highest artistic price to keep it. Yet his presence was necessary, and his contribution during the Chicago renaissance was valuable.

Daniel Burnham was born in Henderson, New York, in 1846, and came to Chicago with his family in 1855. He studied at Snow's Swedenborgian Academy and at Central High School. He managed to graduate in 1865 with an extremely poor record, distinguishing himself only in freehand drawing. He failed the entrance examinations for Harvard and Yale. All his life, he once said, he felt the lack of mental training at college age. But it must be recorded here that Burnham was a man of genuine vision and originality. His failure in schoolwork was a personal matter. His failure to maintain the standards that produced the Chicago Plan of 1895 was in large part, however, the failure of a national culture.

Burnham started his career in 1868 as a clerk in a retail store, but he hated the work and was convinced that he had no ability to insure progress in it. He had felt a bent for architecture when

---

molished); apartment building, 1882, 3200 South Prairie Avenue; Scoville Building, 1884–85, 619–31 West Washington Boulevard; Illinois Central suburban stations, 1886, Thirty-ninth Street and Forty-third Street (demolished); Selz, Schwab and Company factory, 1886–87, Superior and Roberts streets. This last structure was one of the few architecturally worth-while factories of the latter nineteenth century. The continuous piers, carried without break to the top of the parapet, dominate the severely simple façade. The extreme architectonic economy reflects the structural economy: the factory cost only 5½ cents per cubic foot.

For extended analyses and illustrations of many of Adler and Sullivan's commissions up to the Auditorium see Morrison, *op. cit.*, pp. 52–78, 111–16, 294–300, 321–27.

he left high school. As a consequence he entered the office of William Le Baron Jenney (then a partner of the short-lived firm of Loring and Jenney) in the same year. But a curious restlessness drove him out in a short time. He went to Nevada with a mining expedition which failed. He returned to Chicago, ran for state senator, and was defeated. He tried architecture again, establishing a partnership with Gustave Laureau in 1871. The Fire ruined them, and Laureau left town.

Finally, Burnham's father took a hand in this disordered career. In 1872 he placed him as a draftsman in the firm of Carter, Drake and Wight, widely known and successful Chicago architects. He came to admire Peter B. Wight, an eminent Gothic Revivalist, who taught him the practical details of design and aroused in him an appreciation for scholarship. There is some possibility that Wight may have had the worst kind of influence on him.

The opportunity and the association that Burnham needed came in 1872, when he met John Wellborn Root. The partnership they formed in 1873 proved to be another highly productive example of architectural symbiosis. Root possessed a creative technical and artistic talent of the highest order. Burnham, an affable and friendly man, proved an excellent salesman and organizer. When the new office started business, it had one draftsman. The second one the partners hired was William Holabird, the third, Clinton J. Warren.

Burnham proved to be a good executive, and the new business began to grow. He did little designing, but he thoroughly mastered the technical, utilitarian, and financial aspects of building. "Uncle Dan was an impresario"—such was Frank Lloyd Wright's sharp but friendly summation of his ability. But his sense for business was a valuable factor, so long as there was creative talent to give it aesthetic expression. "He considered it was his highest duty," A. N. Rebori wrote, "to permit the structure to serve in the most economical manner possible the functions for which it was intended."[14]

14. "The Architecture of Burnham and Root," *Architectural Record*, XXXVIII, No. 1 (July 1915), 62; quoted in Charles H. Moore, *Daniel Hudson Burnham, Architect, Planner of Cities*, I, 26.

The organizing and business ability which Burnham demonstrated in the amazing rise of his firm brought about his election as chief of construction for the World's Fair of 1893 and, after Root's death, chief consulting architect. During the work on the Fair most of the business of Burnham's office was handled by Dwight Perkins. The Fair and Root's death proved Burnham's undoing. One great building more, and he succumbed to the new eclecticism. He tried to persuade Wright to join him in the exploitation of the classical fashion. It was fortunate for architecture all over the world that Wright gave the answer he did—"I'm afraid it's too late now, Uncle Dan."

JOHN WELLBORN ROOT

Richardson, Sullivan, and Wright are always regarded as the great triumvirate of American architecture. If a fourth were to be added, the choice would waver between Root and Jenney. Root's death at the age of forty-one was a calamity. In addition to his talent as a designer, he knew where the structural art ought to be going, and he had the courage, idealism, and conviction to keep it to its path. As a philosopher of the new movement in architecture, he was second only to Sullivan, but he often spoke with greater force and clarity than his more widely read colleague.

Root was born at Lumpkin, Georgia, in 1850. His youth, like his talent, was the direct opposite of Burnham's. He was destined for some kind of artistic career: he started the serious study of drawing at the age of seven, and of the piano at the age of twelve. When Sherman's army captured his native town, the family was driven out. John was sent to England with Robert T. Wilson, a business associate of his father, Sidney Root. At the age of fourteen he began to attend a school in Liverpool, where he took special courses in architecture and music. His precocity expanded: a lively interest in nature was followed by enthusiasm for the whole domain of art. The depth and breadth of Root's interests seem to have been established at high-school age.

In 1866 he returned to New York and entered New York Uni-

17. AUDITORIUM BUILDING, 1887–89 ADLER AND SULLIVAN

Perhaps Chicago's truest and greatest monument, at the northwest corner of Michigan Avenue and Congress Street. It is now occupied by Roosevelt College. (*Chicago Architectural Photographing Co.*)

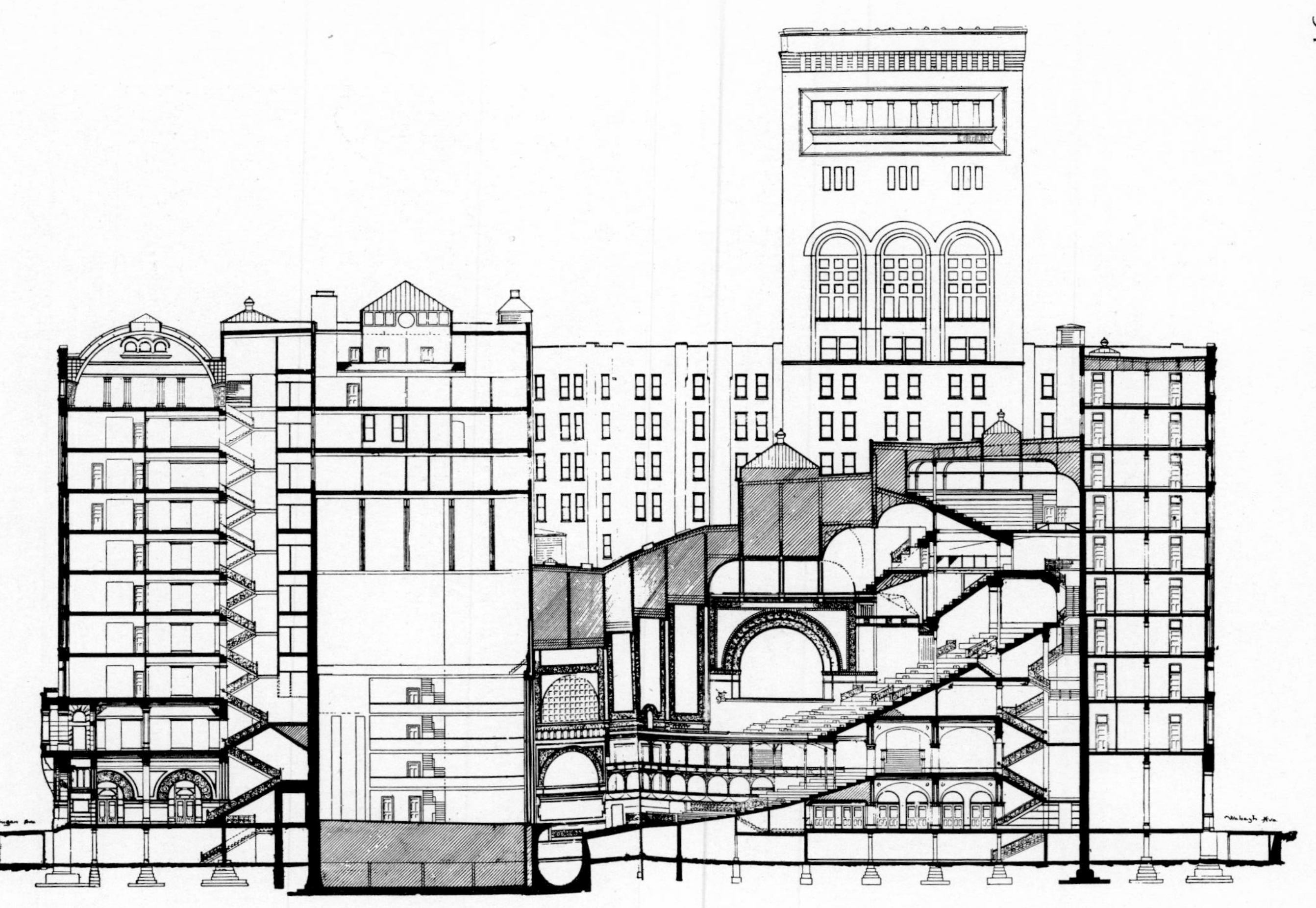

18. AUDITORIUM BUILDING, 1887–89 — ADLER AND SULLIVAN

Longitudinal section. The hotel block is at the Michigan Avenue end (*left*), the theater in the center, and the office block at the Wabash Avenue end (*right*). (*From "Inland Architect and News Record."*)

19. AUDITORIUM HOTEL, 1887–89 ADLER AND SULLIVAN

The main lobby. (*Chicago Architectural Photographing Co.*)

20. AUDITORIUM HOTEL, 1887–89 ADLER AND SULLIVAN

Restaurant and bar. (*Chicago Architectural Photographing Co.*)

21. AUDITORIUM HOTEL, 1887–89 ADLER AND SULLIVAN

Second-floor lobby. (*Chicago Architectural Photographing Co.*)

22. AUDITORIUM HOTEL, 1887–89 ADLER AND SULLIVAN

Main dining-room. (*Chicago Architectural Photographing Co.*)

23. AUDITORIUM THEATER, 1887–89 ADLER AND SULLIVAN

Orchestra and balcony. (*Chicago Architectural Photographing Co.*)

24. AUDITORIUM THEATER, 1887–89 ADLER AND SULLIVAN

View toward the stage. (*Chicago Architectural Photographing Co.*)

25. FIRST LEITER BUILDING, 1879 — William Le Baron Jenney

Now the Morris Building, on the northwest corner of Wells and Monroe streets. The exterior of the first story has been extensively remodeled. (*William Malm.*)

26. TROESCHER BUILDING, 1884 — ADLER AND SULLIVAN

Now the Chicago Joint Board Building, at 15 South Market Street, after many changes of owner and name. (*Commercial Photographic Co.*)

27. WILLOUGHBY BUILDING, 1887 — LEROY BUFFINGTON

Northwest corner of Jackson Boulevard and Franklin Street. (*Kaufmann & Fabry.*)

28. HOME INSURANCE BUILDING, 1883–85 WILLIAM LE BARON JENNEY

The first building of framed or skeletal construction and hence the first true skyscraper, the Home Insurance stood on the southwest corner of La Salle and Adams streets. It was demolished in 1931. (*Commercial Photographic Co.*)

29. CHAMBER OF COMMERCE BUILDING, 1888–89 BAUMANN AND HUEHL

Formerly at the southeast corner of La Salle and Washington streets; demolished in 1926. (*From "Industrial Chicago."*)

30. CHAMBER OF COMMERCE BUILDING, 1888–89 BAUMANN AND HUEHL

The interior light well or court. (*Commercial Photographic Co.*)

31. SECOND LEITER BUILDING, 1889–90 — WILLIAM LE BARON JENNEY

Now the main Sears Roebuck Store, at the southeast corner of State and Van Buren streets. (*Commercial Photographic Co.*)

32. FAIR STORE, 1890–91 WILLIAM LE BARON JENNEY

On the north side of Adams Street from State to Dearborn. (*Commercial Photographic Co.*)

versity in the same year. His record as a student was superior; in addition, he distinguished himself in drawing, in playing the piano and organ, and in composing music. He graduated in 1869 with a B.S. in civil engineering—the best training for an architect in the nineteenth century. He was a draftsman in the office of the New York architect Renwick—another Gothic Revivalist—during the years 1869–70. The influence of Renwick lasted, for Gothic details appeared in some of Root's work up to his death. He moved to the office of an architect named Snooks in 1870, staying for about a year.

Root went to Chicago in 1871 and entered the office of Carter, Drake and Wight, who hired him on the basis of a large portfolio of his plans, sketches, and renderings. It was in this office that he met Burnham. The latter, always ambitious, had now become energetic and practical. Root was lazy, a dreamer, the "artistic" soul who loved to spend money but who always managed to get the job done. The two men complemented each other professionally, but their partnership was as much based on a strong mutual affection. Burnham's influence saved Root from dilettantism and kept him purposeful and confident.

For Root existence in Chicago was divided between the exacting routine of keeping a new office going during the depression of 1873 and a lively plunge into the musical and theatrical life of the community. He was constantly involved in amateur play-producing, concerts, and recitals. He achieved a semiprofessional status in his avocation by reviewing concerts and operas for the *Chicago Tribune*. Meanwhile, the number of commissions slowly increased. For the first eight years the work of the new firm consisted largely of residences. Commercial work came with the Montauk Block (1882), their first big commission. After that date the office was flooded, and success was assured.

In 1882 Root married Dora Louise Monroe, his second wife, and the sister of Harriet Monroe, who became one of the most important individuals in the development of the American poetic renaissance. Her contribution to poetry is widely known; her biography of her brother-in-law is not, however, although it remains the only comprehensive source of information about the life and thought of one of America's greatest architects. Root's architectural philosophy is almost as important as the buildings he designed, yet there has been no extensive consideration of it since Harriet Monroe's biography was published in 1896. With the exception of Sullivan, he was the only architect in the nineteenth century who clearly and fully understood the nature, importance, and purpose of the structural art in an age of mechanized industry.

For all Root's attachment to Romanesque forms and Gothic details, he considered it fortunate that America had no native artistic precedents comparable to those of Europe. She was free, he thought, to create her own architecture, and he believed steadfastly that she would. He aligned himself with the growing movement in the nineteenth century toward honesty in the expression of an organic form. The basic ideas of modern architecture are fully anticipated in Root's papers and addresses.[15]

On the subject of style and its relation to the whole cultural milieu, he discovered the important truth early in his career. "To rightly estimate an essentially modern building," he wrote, "it must not be viewed solely from an archaeological standpoint. . . . Whenever in the world there was a period or style of architecture worth preserving, its inner spirit so closely fitted to the age wherein it flourished, that the style could not be fully preserved, either by the people who immediately succeeded it, or by us after many years. . . . Our architecture if it is good will fit us. . . . The object of all this study of architectural styles must be to acquire from former times the spirit in which our predecessors worked; not to copy what they did. . . . Where architects faithfully follow out the logic of a predetermined theory of their building, they have purity of style."[16]

Root demanded a rational and empirical attitude toward the structural art. He was deeply opposed to the literal use of historical styles, since he was convinced that sound formal solutions could come only from the inherent elements of the struc-

15. Unless another source is indicated, the following quotations are from unpublished papers formerly in the possession of Harriet Monroe and quoted in part in her biography of Root.

16. Quoted in Harriet Monroe, *John Wellborn Root*, pp. 63–64.

tural-utilitarian-human problem with which the architect has to deal in the matter of design. In this respect reason plays a greater part in architecture than in any other art, but imagination is essential after reason has defined the problem and determined its practical solution. Style, in the best sense of the word, would arise only in this way.

In his own words: "Styles grow by the careful study of all the conditions which lie about each architectural problem, and thus while each will have its distinct differentiation from all the others, broad influences of climate, of national habits and institutions will in time create the type, and this is the only style worth considering. . . . The particular thing chosen for the given purpose shall be the best fitted for that purpose—shall in short grow out of it. This is as obvious as to say that a man's exterior form shall be the result of his interior structure."[17] One could hardly find a closer parallel to Sullivan's organic theory.

Root insisted on a fully functional approach to the structural art. The architect must deal rationally and analytically with a large number of physical, economic, social, and psychological factors: the town, the community, the nature and location of the street, climate, orientation, quality of air, available materials and supply of labor; and, if a residence, with the personalities, habits, activities, and vocations of those who will live in it. And, finally, there is the necessity—which we have yet to recognize—of correlating the form of a building with those around it. But, after all the functional and practical considerations, it is an act of creative imagination which turns building into the *art* of architecture. What results is not this style or that; it is *style*, if we must use the term.

In describing the aesthetic qualities of a finished building, Root employed an ingenious metaphor. He compared the characteristics of a fine building to those of a cultivated man. The criteria by which he tested both were Repose, Refinement, Self-containment, Sympathy (that is, an organic and unified relationship to the milieu), Discretion, Knowledge (that is, the reflection of its designer's practical and aesthetic knowledge),

17. *Ibid.*, p. 69.

Urbanity, and Modesty.[18] They are abstractions, but the buildings themselves as well as subsequent papers show that Root understood them well in their concrete dimensions.

Root was well aware of the decadence of architecture in the latter half of the nineteenth century, and he consequently realized that freedom from idolatry of the past was a primary condition of progress. "Architecture," he wrote in 1888, "devotes itself to sensation making. Renaissance follows Renaissance so fast that the new birth never gets past the teething age, and dies before we know the color of its eyes or what its form and complexion would have been. . . . Within the memory of the youngest of us, architectural creations have twice over embodied the whole history of architectural development from Hiram to Norman Shaw."[19]

But a genuine American art can grow up and flourish only if we can rediscover what art, and particularly architecture, truly is. "Every work of fine art is the expression of one dominating idea. . . . It is the dominance of one leading quality over others which is the absolute test of the merit of any work, as it is the law which creates what we call 'style.' . . . The style . . . must not be understood to be . . . a thing of exterior form alone. It lies far deeper. It is the life and existence of the work. As far as material conditions permit it to be possible, a building designated for a particular purpose should express that purpose in every part. The purpose may not be revealed by conventional means, but it must be so plainly revealed that it can be escaped by no appreciative student. . . . The great art work is that which expresses the same intention by less obvious but more inherently significant means—means vital in themselves—the sweep of roof lines—the general repose of mass—the delicacy and grace of ornament—the generosity and openness of aspect. What has just been said indicated another essential characteristic of all true art work—moderation."[20] Thus the true expression

18. "Style," *Inland Architect and Builder*, VIII, No. 10 (January, 1887), 99–101; quoted in Monroe, *op. cit.*, p. 79.

19. "Broad Art Criticism," *Inland Architect and News Record*, XI (February, 1888), 3.

20. *Ibid.*, p. 5.

of functionalism lies in simplicity, directness, and moderation.

The great architectural problem, as Root saw it, was to develop a continuous architectural expression, through mass and structure, of the age of machinery, steam power, and large-scale industry. With surprising acuteness he saw the problem of the arts in a mechanized industrial society and how they would have to meet the challenge of the machine. But the development of a style would not occur as the result of some arbitrary fiat. "We must grant that . . . architecture must normally express the conditions of life about and within it, not in a fragmentary and spasmodic way, but in the mass and structure; the life of the building in large and comprehensive type. As yet the search for a national or new architectural style is absolutely useless for this purpose. Architectural styles . . . were never discovered by human prospectors. . . . Styles are found truly at the appointed time, but solely by those who, with intelligence and soberness, are working out their ends with the best means at hand, and with scarce a thought of the coming new or national style."[21]

Root not only posed the architectural problem but also presented in detail the best solution the nineteenth century had yet developed. In a masterful technical and aesthetic analysis of the modern office building he summed up the best that his age had said on the structural art. He began with the statement that the culture of his time was predominantly rational and scientific, that its approach to building, then, would be rational, empirical, and systematic rather than intuitive. The technical process of design he outlined in nine steps. (1) Cost: the aim is to produce the most efficient and spacious building within the allowance, which includes the price of land. (2) Floor plan for maximum light: the L-shaped plan with narrow wings makes it possible for all offices to have at least one exposure to natural light. (3) Elevators: for easiest access the elevators are concentrated in two central areas flanking the entrance hall. (4) Service facilities: heating and ventilating equipment, electrical conduits and outlets (or gas lines), and storage space are located

21. "A Great Architectural Problem," *Inland Architect and News Record*, XV, No. 5 (June, 1890), 68.

for ease of use, maintenance, and alteration. (5) The optimum height per story is 10 feet 6 inches. (6) Framing and fireproofing of framing members are determined not only by loads but also by conditions of soil. (7) Foundation: the conditions of Chicago soil (that is, any wet, sandy, or spongy soil) require the use of Root's chief structural innovation, a floating raft of concrete reinforced with steel rails, stepped up to receive the wall or the bearing plate at the column foot. (8) Wall construction: the walls should be as open as possible, and their construction involves, among other factors, the temporary support of flanking party walls. (9) Construction of all parts of the building proceeds simultaneously to avoid unequal settlement. When this complex of technical problems has been adequately handled, the architect then turns to his final aesthetic expression.

"All that has been written relates to those portions of the building with which the public at large can have but little interest, but which are the inner and significant principle about which every external aspect must arrange itself. The truest and best forms which this external aspect is to present will be found by a reasonable appreciation of conditions of our civilization, of our social and business life and of our climatic conditions. Even a slight appreciation of these would seem to make it evident . . . that all conditions, climatic, atmospheric, commercial and social, demand for this external aspect the simplest and most straightforward expression. Bearing in mind that our building is a business building, we must fully realize what this means. Bearing also in mind . . . that dust and soot are the main ingredients of our native air, we must realize what this means. Both point the same way. Every material used to enclose the structure we have raised must be, first, of the most enduring kind, and, second, it must be wrought into the simplest forms.

"These buildings, standing in the midst of hurrying, busy thousands of men, may not appeal to them through the more subtle means of architectural expression, for such an appeal would be unheeded; and the appeal which is constantly made to unheeding eyes loses in time its power to attract. In them should be carried out the ideas of modern life—simplicity, stability, breadth, dignity. To lavish upon them profusion of delicate ornament is worse than useless, for this would better be preserved for the place and hour of contemplation and repose. Rather should they by their mass and proportion convey in some large elemental sense an idea of the great, stable, conserving forces of modern civilization.

"Enough has been said to suggest how radically new in type such edifices are, how essential is the difference between the modern and any of the preceding recognized architectural types.

"One result of methods such as I have indicated will be the resolution of our architectural designs into their essential elements. So vital has the underlying structure of these buildings become, that it must dictate absolutely the general departure of external forms; and so imperative are all the commercial and constructive demands, that all architectural detail employed in expressing them must become modified by them. Under these conditions we are compelled to work definitely with definite aims, permeating ourselves with the full spirit of the age, that we may give its architecture true art forms.

"To other and older types of architecture these new problems are related as the poetry of Darwin's evolution is to other poetry. They destroy, indeed, many of the most admirable and inspiring of architectural forms, but they create forms adapted to the expression of new ideas and new aspects of life. Here, vagaries of fashion and temporary fancies should have no influence; here, the arbitrary dicta of self-constituted architectural prophets should have no voice. Every one of these problems should be rationally worked out alone, and each should express the character and aims of the people related to it. I do not believe it is possible to exaggerate the importance of the influence which may be exerted for good or evil by these distinctively modern buildings. Hedged about by many unavoidable conditions, they are either gross and self-asserting shams, untrue both in the material realization of their aims, and in their art function as expressions of the deeper spirit of the age; or they are sincere, noble and enduring monuments to the broad and beneficent commerce of the age."[22]

Root's concern with the theory of architecture and of art in

22. *Ibid.*, pp. 68–71; quoted in Monroe, *op. cit.*, pp. 106–8.

general led to an interest in some of the metaphysical aspects of the subject. In an unpublished paper entitled "A Utilitarian Theory of Beauty" he tried with very questionable success to relate art and science in a logical unity by going to the biological basis of color and form as the basis for the "utility" of the arts to mankind. The idea was certainly organic in a Darwinian sense, but it was a case of stretching the Darwinian theory even beyond the limits of Spencer. This attempt to find a basis for aesthetic values in natural phenomena or external reality lay in the main stream of contemporary thought, finally culminating in Whitehead's impressive synthesis, a systematic and comprehensive organic metaphysics. Other and more fruitful investigations by Root along the same line appeared in a paper entitled "Art of Pure Color." Root had some useful if undistinguished things to say about the importance of color in interior architecture. He also pointed out what even then had come to be a subject of much interest in the graphic arts: the importance to graphic representation of the new work in optics of Helmholtz, Young, Tyndall, and others.[23]

THE EARLY WORK OF BURNHAM AND ROOT

The first important commercial structure designed by Burnham and Root was the Montauk Block, located on the northwest corner of Dearborn and Monroe streets (Fig. 11). It was built in 1882 (a record year—3,113 buildings!) and, for no sound economic or architectural reason, demolished in 1902. The Montauk exerted a considerable influence not only in Chicago but in other cities as well. There was some Romanesque detail in the arched entranceway and in the rusticated and battered masonry of the base, but the general treatment was strikingly original, with little precedent behind it.

The unique element of all its new technical and aesthetic characteristics was the foundation. The stone masonry of the base rested directly on a "floating raft" foundation, developed by Root and used here for the first time, to reduce the height of the individual stepped-up footings of stone under walls and columns.

23. See "Art of Pure Color," *Inland Architect and Builder*, I, No. 6 (July, 1883), 80–82, and *ibid.*, II, No. 1 (August, 1883), 89.

The raft foundation was designed expressly for the soft and compressible soil of the Chicago area, which consists almost entirely of sand and clay interspersed with water pockets. The raft consisted of a slab of concrete about 20 inches thick, reinforced with layers of iron rails to withstand shearing and bending stresses. By means of it the load of the building could be distributed over a large area rather than concentrated on the narrow strip beneath the wall footing. Unit pressures were thus materially reduced, and reasonable uniformity of settlement was assured. Root and the Montauk's owner, Owen F. Aldis, thought of the raft as a steel foundation with a concrete envelope to prevent rusting.

The Montauk Block was a completely fireproof, ten-story brick prism, each story above the first identical with every other. Fireproofing was achieved through hollow-tile subflooring and tile envelopes around the cast-iron columns and wrought-iron floor beams. The use of a continuous terra-cotta band at the sill line of each story heightened the appearance of a rectangular block composed of similar horizontal elements. The windows formed the most striking feature of the building. They were conventional in details but unusually wide and high and closely ranked. Each was capped by a brick lintel in the form of a flat arch. The Montauk was a perfectly functional structure, well proportioned and almost austere in its dignified simplicity. It evolved in part from the American propensity for flat, unadorned wall surfaces.

The high technical and aesthetic excellence of the Montauk was not achieved again until the construction of The Rookery three years later. After the earlier building the work of Burnham and Root took a somewhat different turn, chiefly in the direction of a more open wall and a more pronounced emphasis on revealing the structural characteristics. The exception was a noncommercial building, the Chicago Club, at Michigan Avenue and Van Buren Street, erected in 1882 (the structure collapsed during remodeling in 1929). In this building the architects turned to a bold Romanesque with little modification.

The irregular progress which culminated in The Rookery and

the Monadnock began with the Calumet Building, constructed in 1883–84 on La Salle Street near Adams and demolished in 1913. Although in part a duplication of the Montauk, it represents in one respect an important departure from it. The walls were smooth planes except for narrow horizontal courses at certain stories. But the windows, instead of being separate openings, as in the Montauk, were grouped together in pairs between the piers. The solidity and gravitational tension of masonry construction were reflected in the breadth and massiveness of the piers and spandrels.

The Counselman Building, at the northwest corner of La Salle and Jackson, and the Continental Bank (formerly the Insurance Exchange), at 208 South La Salle Street, were completed in 1884 and 1885, respectively. The Counselman was demolished in 1920, and the Continental in 1912. The first looked toward the Montauk in its flat walls and its absence of ornament. The second, typical of the banking structures designed by Burnham and Root, revealed the continuous piers and grouped openings of the Calumet Building. The present Austin Building at 111 West Jackson Boulevard, originally known as the Phoenix and later the Western Union Building, was completed in 1886. It is a tall, narrow structure, eleven stories in height, with windows paired between slim piers. It is richly ornamented but badly organized. Its profusion suggests The Rookery, but it lacks the latter's unity, clarity, and articulation. The Illinois Bank (La Salle Street? 1886?) involved a long step in the direction of The Rookery. Again the windows were grouped in pairs between masonry piers, but in this case the piers and spandrels were quite narrow, giving much greater openness and surer articulation to the wall. Low, flattened arches spanned the bays at the first and third stories, and the ever present horizontal courses appeared at the top of the first, third, and fifth stories.[24]

The Rookery and the Monadnock Building join the Marshall Field Wholesale Store and the Auditorium as the final monu-

24. All that I have been able to discover of the Illinois Bank is contained in a poor sketch in the *Inland Architect and Builder*, VIII, No. 10 (January, 1887), 2. As a matter of fact, my whole section on the commissions of Burnham and Root between 1882 and 1885 reveals the scarcity of information about them. There are a few illustrations but little written material.

ments of the art of masonry architecture. Many individual buildings, however, show us that other architects were moving in the same direction as Richardson, Sullivan, Burnham, and Root.

SINGLE ACHIEVEMENTS

A little structure on Adams Street still stands to remind us today of the fine work of the early eighties. It is the Dexter Building, 39 West Adams Street, erected in 1883 (Fig. 12). The commission went to Burnham and Root, but the design seems to have been intrusted entirely to Clinton J. Warren, a young member of the firm who early exhibited one of the major talents of the Chicago school. Warren was the school's leading architect of hotels and apartment buildings, reaching his full stature in this field around 1890.[25] He was born in 1860 and came to Chicago in 1879. He entered the office of Burnham and Root in 1880, remained for six years, and founded his own business in 1886. A long list of great hotel buildings secures his reputation.

The Dexter Building reveals Warren's adaptation of Root's taste for continuous piers, windows grouped in pairs between them, and semicircular or full-centered arches. The doubling of the rhythm in the upper two stories is a variation on a common feature of masonry buildings in Chicago. Two characteristics, however, distinguish the Dexter from other comparable work. One is the nearly smooth, uninterrupted plane of the façade up to the seventh story. This, together with the extensive area of glass, takes the main elevation close to the curtain wall of iron or steel framing. The other is the use of shallow reveals and the very slight projection of the piers beyond the spandrels. The result is a nearly impartial expression of horizontal beams and narrow piers and columns. It reveals a tendency toward the neutral wall pattern of a framed building.

The Mallers Building, built in 1884–85 after the plans of John J. Flanders, was an early skyscraper of considerable importance in its day. The twelve-story structure stood on the southwest corner of La Salle and Quincy streets, the highest masonry building at the time of its completion. It was demolished in 1920.

25. See chapter x, the section on "The Work of Clinton J. Warren."

Architecturally it was disfigured by a profusion of ornament—clustered pilasters at the top story, corbels, arches, elaborately decorated spandrels—but it pointed in the right direction. The windows were grouped between continuous piers separating narrow bays, a treatment which gave the building a pronounced vertical accent suggestive of Sullivan's approach to the tall office block. A considerable area of glass was the chief characteristic, aside from its functional interior, that made it a recognizable example of the commercial style.

One of the triumphs of the early period was the Chicago Opera House, designed by Henry Ives Cobb and Charles S. Frost. It was constructed in 1884–85 at the southwest corner of Clark and Washington streets, where it stood until 1912 (Fig. 13). The two designers were partners for only a few years, from about 1884 until 1888. Frost's reputation at the time rested chiefly on the Chicago and North Western Railway Station in Milwaukee, but the Opera House is his only claim to attention today. Cobb was one of the most famous and successful architects in Chicago during the eighties and nineties. He enjoyed an astounding number of commissions given to him from virtually every part of the United States. Aside from the Opera House, his most important work in Chicago was the Newberry Library and the buildings of the University of Chicago.

The Opera House was another combined theater and office block, the theater being in the interior surrounded by a shell of offices. Information about the structural characteristics of this building is entirely lacking, except for the fact that it was of masonry construction. The illustration, however, would seem to suggest precisely the opposite. Exterior bearing members appear to be nonexistent at the first two stories, where there is a floor-to-ceiling envelope of glass divided by narrow mullions. The effect is astonishing and suggests the most advanced contemporary design, in which an uninterrupted sweep of glass surrounds the columns of framed construction. But an analysis of the structure shows that the architects could have achieved this effect even within the sharp limitations of masonry construction.

The elevations throughout the upper eight stories of the Opera House were composed of a succession of alternately wide and narrow piers. The narrow piers had no bearing function. The wide piers, on the other hand, must have been carried to the foundations by stout bearing partitions the outer edges of which project into the glass curtain at the base. The great area of glass, the shallow reveals, and the general light, open, regular quality of the elevations save the structure from a top-heavy appearance. The clarity, sharpness, and rectangularity of walls and over-all profile place the Opera House in the front rank of Chicago buildings in the 1880's.

THE MARSHALL FIELD WHOLESALE STORE

Richardson's influence in Chicago was short lived but profound and extensive. Every important architect in the city except Jenney took something from him. His dominance was broken by the general adoption of steel framing, a structural technique for which he offered no architectonic solution. His greatest achievement and the basis of his influence was the Marshall Field Wholesale Store, which was constructed in 1885–87 on the block bounded by Adams, Wells, Quincy, and Franklin streets (Fig. 14). The store was demolished in 1930 for no intelligible reason, economic or structural, to make way for a parking lot. It would have lasted for more than a century.

The significance of the Marshall Field building has both a positive and a negative aspect. It was an immense block with a total area in plan of 61,750 square feet. It was Richardson's genius that he was able to master so effectively this huge bulk. Yet his mastery was appropriate only to masonry building. "This store," Giedion wrote, "showed Chicago architects how unobtrusively a great volume could be integrated. Richardson injected into this building something of the vitality of the rising city, in a treatment which was full of dignity. The dominance of the windows is emphasized, . . . but the construction is rather conservative. Richardson's massive stone walls belong to an earlier period."[26]

26. *Op. cit.*, p. 294.

All his life Richardson wanted to design a great commercial structure which would reflect the power and organization and boldness of modern commerce. He came closest to it in the Marshall Field building. In the daring simplicity and directness of its huge rectangular prism, in the massive granite walls with their severe economy of detail, in the subtle rhythms of its fenestration, it was a forerunner of the new architecture of industry and commerce, where volume and surface texture and the free expression of structure determine aesthetic effect. Although the fundamental motive of the Field store was Romanesque, the plain and massive stone walls reflected a basic element of American vernacular architecture for over a century. Thus it can be regarded as indigenous, as "an artistic transmutation of elements which had grown out of American life," in Giedion's words.[27] The construction of the store followed that of the typical elevator building: floor and roof loads were carried for the most part on interior cast-iron columns; the outer walls were bearing elements of solid masonry, red granite at the base and sandstone above.

The deep impression made by Richardson's building is best reflected in the ironic and impressionistic metaphors of Sullivan's *Kindergarten Chats:*

"Let us pause, my son, at this oasis in the desert. . . .

"You mean, I suppose, that here is a good piece of architecture for me to look at—and I quite agree with you.

"No; I mean, here is a *man* for you to look at. A man that walks on two legs instead of four, has active muscles, heart, lungs and other viscera; a man that lives and breathes, that has red blood; a real man, a manly man; a virile force—broad, vigorous and with a whelm of energy—an entire male.

"I mean that stone and mortar, here, spring into life, and are no more material and sordid things, but . . . become the very diapason of a mind rich-stored with harmony. . . .

"Four square and brown, it stands, in physical fact, a monument to trade, to the organized commercial spirit, to the power

27. *Ibid.*, p. 285.

and progress of the age, to the strength and resource of individuality and force of character; spiritually, it stands as the index of a mind, large enough, courageous enough to cope with these things, master them, absorb them and give them forth again, impressed with the stamp of large and forceful personality; artistically, it stands as the oration of one who knows well how to choose his words, who has somewhat to say and says it—and says it as the outpouring of a copious, direct, large and simple mind."[28]

THE ROOKERY AND THE MONADNOCK

In sound condition and in full use, The Rookery stands today little affected by the passage of sixty-five years (Fig. 15). Its location, at 209 South La Salle Street, was the site of the temporary city hall and water tank from 1872 to 1884. Half the pigeons in Chicago seem to have selected these structures as a roost; consequently, they came to be known popularly as "The Rookery." When Burnham and Root's building was completed in 1886, the owners, in a moment of practical and humorous good sense, decided to retain the name.

In plan The Rookery is a hollow square surrounding an interior court. Bounded by Quincy Street and an alley on the elevations opposite the thoroughfares (La Salle and Adams streets), it is thus naturally lighted on four sides and in the interior. In construction the building is an unusual mixture of old and new. The exterior walls along La Salle and Adams up to the top story are composed of a series of stout, widely spaced granite columns surmounted by brick piers. At the top story the window rhythm is doubled, and the piers merge with the wall surface. On the periphery of the court, however, and apparently at the first two stories along Quincy Street and the alley the wall load is carried on a series of cast-iron columns joined by wrought-iron spandrel beams—almost true skeletal construction. The wall above the second story on the rear elevations thus appears to be carried on column-and-beam framing. By ex-

28. Louis Sullivan, *Kindergarten Chats*, pp. 28–30.

tending the spandrel beams a few inches beyond the outer edge of the columns, the architects were able to open the wall into a continuous window divided by narrow iron mullions at the second story.[29] This was the first use of what has now become a standard feature of much commercial and industrial architecture. The inner elevations around the court form a remarkably open, simple, nicely proportioned and articulated expression of the iron skeleton which supports them.

The glass-and-iron vault over the inner court and the curving iron stairways at either end provide a beautiful example of such construction, which had become common in nineteenth-century building after the Crystal Palace. The present interior ornament of the court, executed in 1905, was designed by Frank Lloyd Wright. The combination of Root's delicate ironwork and Wright's elaborate gold and ivory decorations provides a rich and luxurious but disciplined effect, suggesting a nineteenth-century counterpart of the magnificence and profuse delicacy of Baroque architecture.

The architectural excellence of The Rookery grows chiefly out of the extraordinary openness of the wall, the airy yet vigorous articulation of the elevations, precise scale and pleasing proportions, and the firm integration of many diverse elements of decorative detail. At the time he designed the building, Root wondered whether the profusion of ornament would stand the test of time. It has, through his sure sense of organization and his subordination of detail to mass and structure. The ornament itself, of course, is far out of touch with the spirit of our time. In spite of its elaborate decorative elements—the arches at the seventh and tenth stories, the corner pinnacles, the five-part horizontal composition, the highly ornamented parapet—The

29. The construction of The Rookery is, in my own opinion, still a matter of controversy. The only framing plan extant is included in an article on the building in the *Engineering Record* of November 3, 1888. This plan shows masonry piers in all four exterior elevations, iron columns only in the interior elevations around the court. An inspection of the building, however, reveals that the piers or columns at the first two stories along Quincy Street and the alley are so greatly reduced in area of cross-section and set so far behind the main wall plane as to suggest heavy iron columns inclosed in a terra-cotta envelope. On the other hand, the author of the *Record* article states explicitly that "the outer wall of the building is entirely of masonry, while the interior wall of the court is a rigid frame work of iron" ("The Rookery," *Engineering Record*, XVIII, No. 23 [November 3, 1888], 273).

33. FAIR STORE, 1891 — William Le Baron Jenney

A portion of the steel and wrought-iron frame during construction, showing how the building was erected in sections. (*From "Industrial Chicago."*)

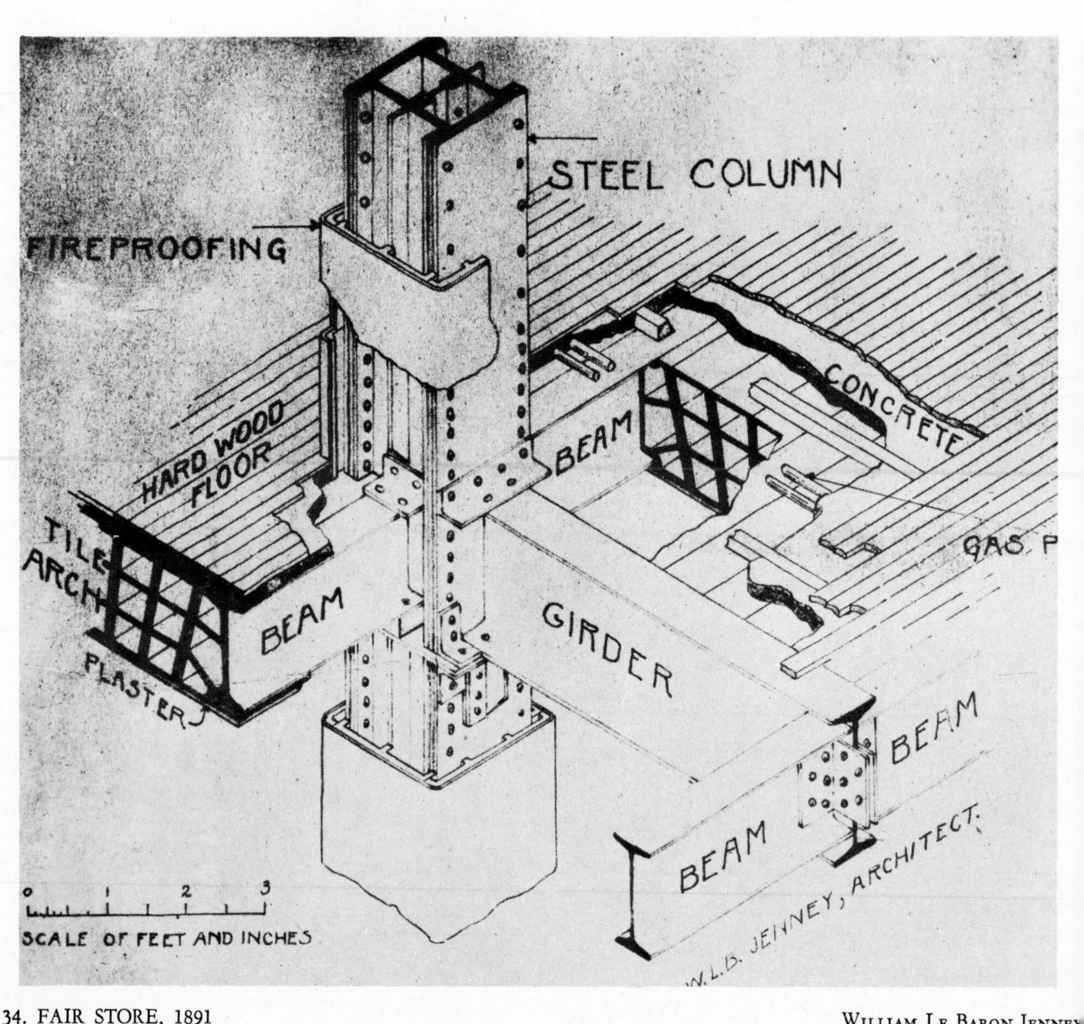

34. FAIR STORE, 1891 — WILLIAM LE BARON JENNEY

Detail of a typical beam-and-column joint, showing connections, forms of structural members, floor construction, fireproofing, and location of pipes and conduits. (*From "Industrial Chicago."*)

35. MANHATTAN BUILDING, 1891 WILLIAM LE BARON JENNEY

431 South Dearborn Street. (*Chicago Architectural Photographing Co.*)

36. South Dearborn Street near Van Buren, looking north. The tall structures (*from right to left*) are the Manhattan, Old Colony, and Fisher buildings. (*Commercial Photographic Co.*)

37. Plymouth Street near Van Buren, looking north. The view shows (*from left to right*) the Manhattan, Old Colony, and Fisher buildings, and a portion of the Great Northern Hotel in the background. The correlation of huge and simple forms is striking. (*Commercial Photographic Co.*)

38. UNITY BUILDING, 1892 CLINTON J. WARREN

127 North Dearborn Street. The iron and steel frame during construction, showing the method of supporting the projecting bays on projections fixed to the spandrel beams. (*From "Industrial Chicago."*)

39. LUDINGTON BUILDING, 1891 — WILLIAM LE BARON JENNEY

1104 South Wabash Avenue. (*Kaufmann & Fabry.*)

40. MORTON BUILDING, 1896 JENNEY AND MUNDIE

538 South Dearborn Street. (*Commercial Photographic Co.*)

41. GREAT NORTHERN HOTEL, 1891 BURNHAM AND ROOT

Formerly at the northeast corner of Dearborn Street and Jackson Boulevard; demolished in 1940. (*Commercial Photographic Co.*)

42. ASHLAND BLOCK, 1892 BURNHAM AND ROOT

Formerly at the northeast corner of Clark and Randolph streets; demolished in 1949 to make way for the new Union Bus Terminal. (*Commercial Photographic Co.*)

43. ASHLAND BLOCK, 1892 BURNHAM AND ROOT

Detail of the street elevations, showing the parapet which replaced the original cornice. (*William Malm.*)

44. WOMAN'S TEMPLE, 1891 BURNHAM AND ROOT

Formerly at the southwest corner of La Salle and Monroe streets; demolished in 1926. (*Commercial Photographic Co.*)

45. MASONIC TEMPLE, 1891 — BURNHAM AND ROOT

Formerly at the northeast corner of State and Randolph streets; demolished in 1939. (*Commercial Photographic Co.*)

46. An old view of Randolph Street, looking east from a point near Clark. The Ashland Block, Garrick Theater, and Masonic Temple appear in succession on the north side. Here we can see most clearly how a new style suddenly sprang up, in the last quarter of the nineteenth century, among the traditional forms of architecture. (*Kaufmann & Fabry.*)

47. MAJESTIC HOTEL, 1893 D. H. BURNHAM AND COMPANY

29 West Quincy Street (*center*). A portion of the Great Northern Hotel appears at the right. (*Commercial Photographic Co.*)

48. RELIANCE BUILDING, 1890, 1895 D. H. BURNHAM AND COMPAN

32 North State Street. Since the first four stories were completed in 1890, the original commission went to Burnham an Root. (*Commercial Photographic Co.*)

Rookery is a direct and powerful revelation of its pier-and-lintel and pier-and-arch construction.

The Monadnock Building differs radically from the older structure in every respect (Fig. 16). It was built in 1889–91 at 53 West Jackson Boulevard. The interior was recently renovated, and its offices are fully occupied today. The original building extended for half a block south along Dearborn Street. In 1893 an addition was constructed after the design of Holabird and Roche, thus extending the building for the rest of the block to Van Buren Street. The addition is of framed construction, and the fenestration differs sufficiently to mark it off clearly from the north half.

The Monadnock is a tremendous unadorned slab two bays wide and sixteen stories high. Its extremely narrow form makes possible an outside exposure for all offices, which are arranged on the periphery of the plan. A stairway rises continuously from bottom to top through openings centrally located in the floors. It is, without question, the ultimate logical step in construction with stone and brick; it remains today the last great building in the ancient tradition of masonry architecture. The walls are of smooth-cut stone at the base and brick above. Cast-iron columns support the inner floor and roof loads. The genesis of the Monadnock's design shows to what extent Root felt that the aesthetic appeal of a building lay in richness of carefully integrated detail as well as in the forceful expression of structure and function. This austere building, consequently, posed a considerable problem for Root's artistic conscience.

Harriet Monroe recorded the struggle in her biography. "For this building," she wrote, "Mr. [Owen] Aldis, who controlled the investment, kept urging upon his architects extreme simplicity, rejecting one or two of Root's sketches as too ornate. During Root's absence of a fortnight at the seashore, Mr. Burnham ordered from one of the draftsmen a design of a straight-up-and-down, uncompromising, unornamented façade. When Root returned, he was indignant at first over this project of a brick box. Gradually, however, he threw himself into the spirit of the thing, and one day he told Mr. Aldis that the heavy sloping lines of an Egyptian pyramid had gotten into his mind as the basis of this design, and that he thought he would 'throw the thing up without a single ornament.' At last, with a gesture whose pretense of disgust concealed a shy experimental interest, he threw on the drawing table of Mr. Dutton, then foreman of the office, 'a design,' says this gentleman, 'shaped something like a capital I—a perfectly plain building curving outward at base and cornice.' This was the germ of the final design, and it provoked much discussion and study in the office."[30] For forty years Montgomery Schuyler was the only critic of architecture who appreciated its greatness.

The technical innovations of the Monadnock—floating raft foundation, continuous bay windows to provide for maximum admission of light, the immense footings to carry the great weight of sixteen stories—reveal that Root's creative powers in structural engineering matched those of the artist-designer. The general appearance of the building almost belies its masonry construction. The projecting bays of the walls with their large glass area give the structure an appearance of weightlessness in spite of its great mass. Stripped of every vestige of ornament save the slight inward curve of the wall at the top of the first story and the outward flare of the parapet, subtly proportioned and scaled, the Monadnock is a severe yet powerfully expressive composition in horizontal and vertical lines. It presents in its relentless exactitude the formal beauty latent in the commercial style, but at the same time it demonstrates the limitations of the old method of construction. "Its expression," Giedion wrote, "derives more from architectonic refinement than from the new potentialities. And heavy masonry walls were not the solution to the problem of the many-storied building. The rather small dimensions of the windows indicated the extent to which they hampered the architect."[31]

The Monadnock is not the embodiment of a new technical-artistic synthesis, as the new architecture of iron framing had already come to be. Yet Root's building offers one of the most exciting aesthetic experiences our commercial architecture can

30. *Op. cit.*, p. 141. 31. *Op. cit.*, p. 296.

show. The precisely logical relationship between form and function has the appeal of mathematical rigor: it is the widest generalization free of contradiction. In this respect Walter Behrendt found the building highly significant. "In its rigid functionalism," he wrote, "demonstrating a new conception, it became a landmark of modern building: the architect, as an artistic personality, steps back behind the commission given him by society. In an act of self-denial, he puts his individual forces into service for common needs, arising from the new social evolution. In this attitude is manifested the truth that building is a social art. The consequence of this conception . . . is to bring building again into a reasonable organic relation to the actual social and economic world, thereby re-establishing that indispensable identity between the content and the form of life, which is missed in the works of those who have turned their backs on their time."[32]

THE AUDITORIUM

The reputation of Adler and Sullivan and, for that matter, of Chicago itself was made and secured by the Auditorium Building. The largest and most complex building in the country at the time of its construction, it was built from civic and aesthetic motives rather than commercial. The sheer size of the Auditorium makes even more impressive the extraordinary architectural and technical skill which entered into its design and construction. Ten stories in height, it extends the entire block along Congress Street from Michigan to Wabash Avenue. Its total area in plan is 63,350 square feet; the substructure required 28,000 cubic yards of excavation; the foundation contains 22,000 linear feet of steel rail; the total weight of the finished structure is 101,000 tons. Three years (1887–89) were needed to complete the construction, the final cost of which was $3,145,291. The whole country could show nothing grander.

The building embraces much more than a theater. The auditorium proper, with a seating capacity of 4,237, occupies the center portion of the structure; the Wabash Avenue (west) end

32. Walter C. Behrendt, *Modern Building*, p. 120.

is a typical commercial office block; the Michigan Avenue (east) end is a hotel (Figs. 17 and 18). The problem of integrating this vast complex of separate elements within uniform elevations taxed the ingenuity of Adler and Sullivan to the utmost. That they succeeded is attested not only by the appearance of the building but by the fact that it is in good condition and, except for the theater, in active use today.

The forerunner of this extraordinary venture into the presentation of dramatic and musical performances was the Chicago Opera Festival, whose productions were given in the auditorium of the Grant Park Exposition Building, erected in 1873 after the plans of W. W. Boyington. Ferdinand W. Peck, sponsor of the opera festivals at the Exposition, in 1885 projected the idea of a permanent opera house which would include a civic center for musical festivals, symphony concerts, dance programs, balls and other social functions, and political conventions. To make the investment financially possible, Peck proposed the addition of office and hotel space around the theater. To prosecute this ambitious program, the Chicago Opera Association was founded in 1886. The commission for the design of its building went to Adler and Sullivan in the same year.

The first projects were more ornate than the final design, and they were constantly modified at conferences with Peck and the directors.[33] The decisive change in the plans of the Auditorium came as the result of the influence of Richardson's Marshall Field store. Both Sullivan and Peck had a profound admiration for the earlier building; in addition, the board of the Auditorium Association saw many possible economies in the adoption of its simplicity. Fortunately for architecture everywhere, Sullivan abandoned his propensity for elaborate ornament and concentrated on the architectonic effect of mass, texture, and the proportioning of large and simple elements. The final over-all plans were completely early in 1887, and construction began immediately. Often the building gangs worked in shifts, continuing through the night under electric floodlights.

33. For earlier designs see Morrison, *op. cit.*, Pls. 12 and 13, p. 328. The greater part of my discussion of the Auditorium is based on Morrison's clear, detailed, and comprehensive analysis (*ibid.*, pp. 85–110).

The exterior walls of the Auditorium and all partitions dividing the theater from offices and hotel are load-bearing members of solid masonry. Brick was used throughout, with granite facing at the first three stories, limestone above. The load on the foundations is continuous rather than distributed over separate piers. The foundations, concrete reinforced with timber and steel rails, deliver a unit pressure of 4,000 pounds per square foot to the soil beneath them. The total settlement of the building under load was 18 inches, which necessitated the use of lead-pipe connections to absorb the strain on iron pipe and conduit. Between structural walls the interior load falls on isolated spread footings of the typical pyramid shape. The great problem in the design of foundations was occasioned by the tower on the Congress Street side. This structure weighs 15,000 tons, and its area in plan of 2,870 square feet is carried on a foundation 6,700 square feet in area. Thus unit pressures under the tower were increased to 4,480 pounds per square foot. Adler supported it on a massive raft 5 feet thick, reinforced with two layers of timbers, three of rails, and three of I-beams.

To avoid increased settlement of the tower after construction, Adler used what amounted to a kind of crude prestressing of the supporting soil. He forced artificial settlement of the tower foundation by loading it with brick and pig iron to the extent necessary to secure maximum settlement. As construction progressed, he decreased the artificial load by an amount equal to the weight of the portion of the tower just completed. This Gargantuan effort was rendered unnecessary by Adler's invention of caisson foundations for the Stock Exchange Building in 1893.

But the tower foundation was not the end of Adler's special worries over the Auditorium. The basement floor below the stage lies about 7 feet below mean water level in Lake Michigan. Waterproofing concrete by means of paint had been used before, but waterproofing it against considerable pressure was an unprecedented difficulty. Adler met the problem in his characteristic way, which was direct, ingenious, and perfectly empirical. He designed a laminated floor made up of alternate layers of concrete, asphalt, and asphalt-saturated felt, counterweighted with additional concrete and rails to offset the upward-acting hydraulic pressure.

As in the Central Music Hall and the Chicago Opera House, the theater of the Auditorium at no point projects to the streets, being surrounded by a continuous volume containing offices, hotel rooms, and public facilities (Fig. 18). The fenestration of the building is thus determined by the hotel and office blocks. The entrance to the theater is marked by a triple arch on the Congress Street elevation close to Wabash Avenue. It is subdued in treatment and hardly as spectacular as the hotel entrance on the Michigan Avenue side, with the heavy balcony on corbels above it. Elsewhere on the street elevations the base is a massive wall of huge, rough-cut granite blocks.

The general design of the walls was derived in part from the Marshall Field Wholesale Store. The three-story base is of heavily rusticated granite blocks. This, together with the stout piers, narrow windows, and heavy lintels, conveys an effect of great force and dignity. The four middle stories fall under high semicircular arches each spanning the whole bay. The next two stories are under arches of half the span of the lower, and the openings of the top story are rectangular. The wall above the base rises in a rhythmic succession of continuous stone piers, relatively narrow compared to the window openings. The rhythm developed by piers and arches is doubled at the ninth story, then tripled at the top. A simple stone cornice brings the whole upward motion to a clean stop. The elevations form a beautiful illustration of Sullivan's unique feeling for harmony, scale, and proportion. The rich but disciplined texture of the wall has the quality of a musical composition: there are four basic, repetitive rhythms, each representing a slight variation on the other, but all positively integrated into a harmonious whole.

Sullivan treated the elevations of the building as plastic objects, to be molded according to his feeling about the structure, as he did in the case of many buildings throughout his career. ' The disposition of the elements in the façade,'' Morrison wrote, ''is . . . a formal and artificial one, and it certainly does not correspond to the internal functional divisions . . . of the building. On the other hand, the exterior design admirably expresses the heavy masonry construction, and in its large simplicity, its absence from merely trivial or 'picturesque' outbreaks of surface ornament or irregularities of silhouette, it goes far beyond the building of its era in achieving a truly monumental form."[34]

The only interruption to the uniformity of the elevations is the tower on the Congress Street side. It stands seventeen stories high, its south elevation nearly flush with the main wall of the building. Below the cornice the tower has the same pattern as the building wall, but it is slightly projected beyond the plane of the wall. The cornice cuts across the tower, thus detaching the upper portion from the main mass. The result is that the tower is partly separated from and partly merged with the building proper. It is not the completely satisfactory treatment of the difficult problem of mastering a functional necessity. The tower was constructed to house the hydraulic machinery for the stage. Above this space, for twenty years, were the offices of Adler and Sullivan and of Sullivan alone.

The Auditorium Hotel inclosed the theater on the Michigan Avenue and Congress Street sides. The average depth of this L-shaped honeycomb of rooms and facilities is only 45 feet, yet it contained a lobby, smoking-room, parlor, restaurant, dining-room, banquet hall, bar, four hundred guest rooms, kitchens, and service rooms.[35] The entrance on Michigan Avenue opened into a rich lobby with a marble mosaic floor and a dado of Mexican onyx (Fig. 19). The decoration of structural details consisted of gilded plaster relief of intricate foliated pattern. (The relief still remains, but it has been painted over.) With respect to ornament the bar was an excellent example of Sullivan's originality: it reflected his rebellion against tradition, his fertility of invention, and his astonishing fluency in trying to develop a new ornamental vocabulary (Fig. 20).

34. *Op. cit.*, p. 95.

35. Since the purchase of the Auditorium Building by Roosevelt College in 1946, the old hotel facilities have been progressively transformed into classrooms, laboratories, and offices.

The second floor of the hotel contained the main lounge, reached by a stairway with onyx paneling, gilded plaster relief, and wrought-iron stair rails (Fig. 21). The mosaic floors of the landings were composed of an intricate profusion of detail and a great richness of color, all thoroughly disciplined and harmonized. It was the lyrical element of nineteenth-century architecture developed almost to the point of Baroque lavishness.

The dining-hall on the tenth floor ran the whole length of the Michigan Avenue front, with a view of Grant Park and the lake to the east (Fig. 22). The area is covered with a curved vault which springs directly from the floor level. The vault is carried on five arch trusses covered by panels decorated in plaster relief centered around electric-light bulbs. Smaller dining-rooms at the ends were separated from the main room by columns carrying a rich frieze. The tympana of the arches over the frieze were adorned by mural paintings.

What was formerly the hotel kitchen is a remarkable feat of construction. It is structurally independent of the main building, being carried on wrought-iron trusses spanning the theater stage. Bridges connected it with the dining-rooms. The special banquet hall was handled in the same way, being supported over the theater by trusses. Again Sullivan's use of decorative electric lighting showed his power of integrating utilitarian necessities into a formal architectural whole.

The office block on Wabash Avenue, still much as it was when completed, contains 136 offices. This section is separated from the theater by a thick masonry bearing wall. The sixth-floor corridor, however, was used as an auxiliary entrance and exit for the upper galleries of the theater, to which it is joined by bridges. The recital hall above the upper galleries was reached from the seventh-floor corridor. Elevators serve all the offices.

But the offices and hotel of the Auditorium Building are incidentals; the theater is the main element of the structure. Its over-all area, including foyers, vestibules, stage, and facilities, is nearly half the area in plan of the whole structure. The box-office vestibule on Congress Street leads to the ground-floor foyer, from which tunnels lead to the front rows of the orchestra floor. The rear rows of the orchestra floor are reached from the second-floor foyer. The same arrangement of tunnels and foyers at two levels serves the balcony.

The main floor of the theater was designed according to acoustical principles rather than sight lines, the total rise of 17 feet from front to rear being more than necessary for unobstructed vision (Fig. 23). This upward-curving surface, together with the elliptical vault of the theater ceiling and the lateral breaks in the ceiling, provides virtual acoustical perfection. The lateral breaks cover the arches and house the ventilating ducts. The arches are light arch trusses hung from heavy horizontal trusses 118 feet long and carrying a total load of 660 tons. The general form of the vault is that of a succession of four elliptical cylinders whose axes become progressively longer toward the rear. The breaks or projections divide the successive vaults. Most of the reflected waves can thus be diffused over the whole theater, while the breaks interrupt the waves which have traveled farthest and thus prevent annoying echoes at the rear of the theater. But the elimination of echoes and reverberation is chiefly a matter of the height of the vault, which Adler carefully calculated to this end. The architects of the Chicago Civic Opera House, constructed in 1928, followed the design of the Auditorium as the acoustical standard. Adler was forty years ahead of his time.

The balcony is somewhat longer than the main floor. The upward curve of the balcony floor, amounting to 40 feet, was determined by the same acoustical principles after which the orchestra level was designed. The two galleries above the balconies are reached by stairways from the rear balcony, from the sixth-floor office corridor, and by means of bridges and tunnels in the case of the second gallery. The galleries are supported on cast-iron columns and wrought-iron trusses so located as not to interfere with sight lines.

The proscenium arch of the stage rises in an elliptical curve bordered by murals on a gold ground (Fig. 24). The proscenium wings, which spread out at an angle from the curtain, are decorated with fanlike trellises and gilded plaster relief. The organ grill opens at the left, the organ itself standing in a separate inclosure north of the stage. It was the most complete instrument in the world at the time of installation. Although the stage is the center of attraction, the great arches of the vault form the dominant architectural motive. Their grand sweep is covered with intricate ornament and studded with electric lights. "Rarely has there been such a wedding of large and majestic simplicity with refined and subtle detail"—in Morrison's words.[36]

Adler developed an ingenious method for reducing seating capacity for solo recitals. On the advice of Augustin Daly, he devised a means of closing off the galleries and the rear third of the upper balcony by making the ceilings above these areas a series of hinged panels which could be dropped by windlasses into the position of partitions. But this device resulted in a deterioration of acoustical properties, and shortly after the initial use soloists said they preferred to sing or play to the whole theater volume even with the galleries empty.

The mechanical equipment of the stage was the most complete and refined at the time of installation. Adler went to Europe to study the best facilities on the Continent, but he introduced radical changes into European techniques to suit American practice. An important innovation was the construction of the stage in sections which could be lifted by hydraulic machinery. In this way the stage could be banked for choral concerts and the like. Lowered flat, overlaid with hardwood, and opened to its fullest extent, it made a ballroom capable of accommodating eight thousand people. There is a great amount of mechanical and hydraulic equipment above and below stage, which is still one of the largest and best equipped in the country. With few exceptions, there is nothing like it in theaters devoted to opera and drama.

There were no consulting engineers on the Auditorium. Except for minor details, Adler did the whole job. He belongs, on the merit of this building, with the great engineers of the nineteenth century—world figures—Eiffel, Roebling, Eads, Paxton.

36. *Op. cit.*, p. 104.

On the Auditorium the later success of Adler and Sullivan was built and, in good measure, the later fame of the Chicago school and of the city itself. Like the Monadnock, it was the high point, in an age of mechanized industrial techniques, of masonry architecture. It brought the old system of construction to a close and pointed to the new structural art growing up around it.

CHAPTER IV

Jenney and the New Structural Technique

THE GROWTH OF IRON FRAMING

THE revolution which brought about the most radical transformation in the structural art since the development of Gothic architecture in the twelfth century was the invention of complete iron framing or skeletal construction. To trace the evolution of the iron frame in Chicago takes us back ten years before the completion of the Auditorium. In 1879 the first Leiter Building of William Le Baron Jenney was erected at the northwest corner of Wells and Monroe streets (Figs. 3 and 25). It was originally five stories in height, but two more were added in 1888. Now the Morris Building, with a base spoiled by "modernization," it still stands in good condition. This structure is of a special kind of mill construction which marks the important intermediate step between James Bogardus' invention of 1848 and Jenney's achievement of full framing in 1883–85.

The first Leiter is very nearly a glass box. The interior floor and roof load is carried on timber girders supported by cast-iron columns. The brick piers, however, are not essential bearing members. The outer floor beams are carried to iron columns immediately inside the piers, thus freeing the latter from interior loads and reducing them to fireproof envelopes. The piers thus support only themselves and serve chiefly to inclose the building in its glass and cast-iron envelope. Since they are not bearing members, Jenney was able to reduce them to very narrow width. "Had the wall columns been inserted in the piers," Randall writes, "and had three more columns been added, the construction would have been essentially skeleton construction."[1]

In appearance the Leiter Building is a series of slender, widely spaced piers and spandrels forming a continuous pattern from base to roof. Each of the large rectangular panels enframed by the brickwork is filled by three windows extending from floor to ceiling and separated by cast-iron mullions, which are continuous from foundation to roof and have a bearing function. The wide openings of glass anticipate the huge "Chicago windows" of the next decade. Devoid of ornament except for an unobtrusive cornice, happily free from the frequent horizontal composition reminiscent of base-shaft-capital treatment of a column, with fine proportions, the Leiter Building exhibits one motive from top to bottom, that of a simple, open, glass-inclosed cage. This little structure was far more daring and original than even the Monadnock.

Adler and Sullivan's small building at 15 South Market Street, constructed in 1884, is a halfway step toward Jenney's achievement in the first Leiter (Fig. 26).[2] The piers are masonry, but the lintels are 8-inch wrought-iron I-beams which carry the spandrels and the sash of the bay above. Thus they anticipate the wall-supporting spandrel beam of skeletal construction. The lunettes at the top story of the Troescher represent the worst that Sullivan did in ornamentation. They spoil an otherwise graceful façade.

The Willoughby Building, 1887, at the northwest corner of Jackson Boulevard and Franklin Street, is essentially a framed building like those constructed by James Bogardus thirty years before its time (Fig. 27). This building was probably designed by Leroy Buffington, who took out a patent on skeletal construction about the time Jenney's Home Insurance Building was completed in 1885. The walls of the Willoughby are composed almost entirely of glass set between cast-iron columns and

1. Frank A. Randall, *History of the Development of Building Construction in Chicago*, p. 89.

2. The building at 15 South Market has had many names, among them the Troescher, the Chicago Journal, the Louis Sullivan, and the Chicago Joint Board Building. It now bears the last one, being the office of the International Ladies Garment Workers Union. It stood as a belated memorial to its architect for a short time around 1945, when it carried his name.

wrought-iron spandrel beams. The ornament obscures what is otherwise an open and graceful pattern of closely spaced, slender piers and large windows.

THE TRUE SKELETON: THE HOME INSURANCE BUILDING

The development of cast-iron framing shows that skeletal construction had been virtually achieved in several buildings prior to the completion of Jenney's Home Insurance Building. The decisive step, however, remained to be taken. This was the reduction of the exterior wall to a mere curtain or envelope which is *supported throughout by the interior framing*. In a framed building the wall not only has no bearing function but it does not even support itself. A finished building of skeletal construction can be reduced to nothing more than a framework covered by glass. Actually a structure like Jenney's skyscraper has no wall in the usual sense of the word but only a succession of vertical and horizontal bands of masonry or weatherproof metal covering the outermost columns and beams.

The revolution which converted a building from a crustacean with its armor of stone to a vertebrate clothed only in light skin occurred in the two years following 1883, when Jenney received the commission for the Chicago office of the Home Insurance Company. Construction began in that year and was completed in 1885. The building stood on the southwest corner of La Salle and Adams streets until its demolition in 1931—the first true skyscraper, the first complete answer to the problem of large-scale urban construction (Fig. 28). This achievement alone would have secured a lasting reputation for Jenney, but it is equally to his credit that he developed a full architectonic expression of his great technical innovation. His revolution was both structural and aesthetic, although the latter aspect did not emerge in its maturity until the completion of the second Leiter Building in 1890.

The construction and functional arrangement of the Home Insurance Building were relatively simple. The frame consisted of serial column-and-beam construction, made up of round cast-iron columns, wrought-iron box columns of built-up section, and wrought-iron I-beams joining them to receive the floor loads. Lintels and mullions, which were continuous, were cast iron. The whole complex was bolted together by means of angles, webs, and gusset plates. The columns were carried on isolated spread footings designed to transmit 4,000 pounds per square foot to the soil. The footings, in turn, rested on reinforced concrete rafts supported by hard-pan clay at 12 feet 6 inches below grade level. The exterior envelope was granite at the first story and brick with sandstone trim above. The building was originally ten stories high, but two more were added in 1890. The granite envelope of the columns at the base carried 18 per cent of the total column load on the periphery, a deviation from full framing which made possible the addition of the two top stories. Above the base all portions of the exterior wall, which was not self-supporting, were carried on shelf angles fixed to the spandrel beams. Thus the outermost floor beam carried not only its portion of the floor load but also one bay of the exterior wall, up to the beam next above it. This method of carrying the outer envelope still remains the standard practice for tall steel- or concrete-framed structures. Without this technique, as a matter of fact, the skyscraper would be an impossibility.[3]

Architecturally the Home Insurance Building did not entirely live up to its great technical importance. The street elevations were in general appearance impartial revelations of the interior frame. One sees that the gravitational thrust of the masonry bearing wall here gave way to the neutral tension of the steel cage, which is neither horizontal nor vertical but simply a honeycomb of rectangular cells. But Jenney obscured the sharp impression his building could have made. The elevations revealed a six-part horizontal composition, employed undoubtedly to interrupt what was thought to be the monotony of a ten-story wall. The corner piers and the continuations of those flanking the entranceway were wide, the rest relatively narrow. All piers carried elaborate capitals at the fourth, seventh, ninth, and twelfth stories. A balcony on corbels over each entrance and

3. For an exhaustive structural analysis of the Home Insurance see Randall, *op. cit.*, pp. 105–7.

a complicated parapet added to the inappropriate excess of other details. The whole composition showed a habitual weakness in Jenney: his inability to free himself, in the design of a big and expensive building, from obsolete theories of ornamentation which the specialists in his office imported from the German schools. It was a curious mixture of great structural vigor and redundant decorative details. It appeared again in the Fair Store and the Manhattan Building, but it was greatly refined in the second Leiter.

The utilitarian advantages of steel framing were enormous and immediately obvious to architects, builders, and owners. First was the possibility of getting rid of a supporting wall, with a consequent reduction in weight and an immense increase in height. The steel necessary to carry a tall building weighs only one-third as much as bearing masonry for an equal number of stories. The virtually unlimited increase in glass area, up to 100 per cent of coverage, allowed the maximum admission of light. The slender columns and wide bays offered greatly increased freedom in the disposition of interior space. Economy in cost of materials together with speed and efficiency of construction convinced even the most skeptical owners of the superiority of steel or wrought-iron framing. In the case of the Home Insurance Building the deciding factor seems to have been the admission of the greatest quantity of natural light available on a narrow, closely built street.

The interesting question for students of architectural history is: To what extent did Jenney consciously seek to develop a new architectural form or the basis of a new style? The answer appears to be that, although he was aware of the aesthetic possibilities or of his own aesthetic achievements, he was not directly concerned with such matters. Elmer C. Jensen, a member of Jenney's office from 1885 until the latter's death in 1907, thinks that Jenney's approach was basically utilitarian. "While [he] felt," Jensen writes, "[that] he was contributing to the making of new architectural forms, that was not his motive. His main purpose was the development of more efficient structural features. My personal opinion is that while he was fully conscious

49. FISHER BUILDING, 1897 D. H. BURNHAM AND COMPANY

343 South Dearborn Street. (*Commercial Photographic Co.*)

50. RAILWAY EXCHANGE BUILDING, 1904 D. H. BURNHAM AND COMPANY

Northwest corner of Jackson and Michigan boulevards. (*Commercial Photographic Co.*)

51. TACOMA BUILDING, 1887–89 HOLABIRD AND ROCHE

Formerly at the northeast corner of La Salle and Madison streets; demolished in 1929. (*Chicago Architectural Photographing Co.*)

52. CAXTON BUILDING, 1889–90 HOLABIRD AND ROCHE

Formerly at 508 South Dearborn Street (*center*); demolished in 1947 to make way for the Congress Expressway. (*Commercial Photographic Co.*)

53. MONADNOCK BUILDING, SOUTH ADDITION, 1893 HOLABIRD AND ROCHE

The southward extension of the original Monadnock, along Dearborn Street to Van Buren. (*Commercial Photographic Co.*)

54. PONTIAC BUILDING, 1891 HOLABIRD AND ROCHE

542 South Dearborn Street. (*Commercial Photographic Co.*)

55. MARQUETTE BUILDING, 1894 HOLABIRD AND ROCHE

140 South Dearborn Street (*right*). (*Commercial Photographic Co.*)

56. OLD COLONY BUILDING, 1894 — HOLABIRD AND ROCHE

407 South Dearborn Street. (*Commercial Photographic Co.*)

57. OLD COLONY BUILDING, 1894 — HOLABIRD AND ROCHE

The north elevation. (*Chicago Architectural Photographing Co.*)

58. The three buildings of the Gage group as they originally appeared. *Left and center:* 30 and 24 South Michigan Avenue, 1898, HOLABIRD AND ROCHE; *right:* 18 South Michigan Avenue, 1898–99, LOUIS SULLIVAN. Four stories were added to Sullivan's building in 1902. (*Chicago Architectural Photographing Co.*)

59. The three buildings of the Gage group as they now appear. Sullivan's design (*on the right*) was originally an eight-story structure; four more were added in 1902. The illustration provides an illuminating set of contrasts: the fine architecture of the Chicago school; the banality of "modern" shop fronts; the dreadful excesses of later work in the two buildings on either side of the center group. (*Chicago Architectural Photographing Co.*)

60. WILLIAMS BUILDING, 1898 Holabird and Roche

205 West Monroe Street. (*Kaufmann & Fabry.*)

61. CABLE BUILDING, 1899 — HOLABIRD AND ROCHE

Now the Hoops Building, at the southeast corner of Wabash Avenue and Jackson Boulevard. (*Commercial Photographic Co.*)

62. McCLURG BUILDING, 1899–1900 HOLABIRD AND ROCHE

Now the Crown Building, at 218 South Wabash Avenue. (*Commercial Photographic Co.*)

63. VICTORIA HOTEL, 1892–93 ADLER AND SULLIVAN

Located in Chicago Heights; now extensively remodeled. (*Chicago Architectural Photographing Co.*)

64. MEYER BUILDING, 1893 — ADLER AND SULLIVAN

Southwest corner of Franklin and Van Buren streets. The original cornice has been replaced by a parapet. (*Chicago Architectural Photographing Co.*)

that his ideas and buildings were developing new forms, his main purpose was to create structural features which increased the effective floor areas and made it possible to secure more daylight within the buildings. . . . I do not recollect that he made any remarks about creating new forms although he did remark that skeleton construction would bring about a revolution in the design of office buildings."[4]

The second Leiter Building is so vigorous a revelation of the new construction that one feels, whether Jenney was consciously aiming at it or not, that he was a master of architectonic form. Before we consider his major achievement, however, the Chamber of Commerce Building deserves attention. It was most immediately and most thoroughly influenced by the Home Insurance office.

THE CHAMBER OF COMMERCE BUILDING

The structure which logically carried forward the development of Jenney's art was not designed by him. The Chamber of Commerce Building, erected in 1888–89 at the southeast corner of La Salle and Washington streets, was the work of Edward Baumann and Harris Huehl (Fig. 29). It was obviously influenced by the Home Insurance and stood as a greatly refined expression of what Jenney was seeking in the earlier building. In this respect it becomes the natural step in the transition from the tentative and partial statement of the Home Insurance to the mature and confident expression of the second Leiter Building. Its demolition in 1926 was a shameless waste of a useful and beautiful achievement. The Chamber of Commerce took the place of the old Board of Trade Building, constructed immediately after the Fire. Thus it had an important symbolic function as well as a utilitarian purpose. It was easily the proudest and most advanced work of structural art at the time of its completion.

The Chamber of Commerce was a fully framed building. Its bolted wrought-iron and steel skeleton rested on a raft foundation made up of several layers of steel rails laid at right angles

4. Communication from Elmer C. Jensen, dated April 13, 1949.

and imbedded in concrete. The total weight of the frame for this thirteen-story structure was 32,000 tons. The frame had an exterior envelope of marble at the base and brick above. The articulation of the wall was remarkable for clarity and precision. The two-story base was a radical departure from the traditional massive and solid stonework, a characteristic of even the Home Insurance. The architects reduced it to glass in large panes fixed between the narrow piers. Except for the arbitrary horizontal division produced by means of continuous courses at the top of the second, fifth, eighth, and twelfth stories, the dominant accent was vertical, the result of continuous piers and slightly recessed spandrels. But, aside from these details and the special but meaningless variation of the elevation at the thirteenth story, the walls were perfectly clear statements of the neutral cage which lay within them. There are other obscuring elements—the rustication at the first five stories, the capricious alteration of the pier width, the capitals on the wide piers at the top of the fifth story, but the over-all treatment of the street elevations revealed a surer mastery of the means of expression than Jenney's building could show.

The unique and striking feature of the Chamber of Commerce was the interior light court extending through the entire height of the building and roofed with glass at the top (Fig. 30). Thus the building was a hollow rectangle in plan. The offices formed a shell or honeycomb around the court, and the corridors were in reality balconies carried on cantilever beams fixed to the columns on the periphery of the court. The elaborate ironwork of the railings was entirely in keeping with the rich quality of the whole structure, with its unusual quantity of costly marble veneer on both interior and exterior.

The Chamber of Commerce justly made a great impression in its day. It would have put to shame most commercial architecture erected up until the late 1920's. Its wanton destruction in 1926 was a serious blow to the cause of fine building. The authors of *Industrial Chicago* were perfectly clear about its position in their own city. "In the matter of light and live air," they wrote, "it is superior to all other buildings, and in strength, equipment and decoration equal to any of them except the Auditorium."[5]

THE SECOND LEITER BUILDING

The second building to house the department store of the Levi Z. Leiter Company was Jenney's triumph. It is now the main Sears Roebuck Store, standing on the southeast corner of State and Van Buren streets, where it was erected in 1889–90 (Fig. 31). Siegel, Cooper and Company owned it originally and sold it to Leiter, from whom it passed to its present owners. In its boldness, vigor, and originality it is one of the most impressive works of commercial architecture the nation can show. Jenney knew exactly what he was doing and never wavered in the execution of his plan.

The Sears Roebuck Store is a huge rectangular prism 402 feet long, eight stories high, and 57,900 square feet in area of plan. The exterior surfacing of columns and spandrels is gray granite, with little irregularity or ornamentation to interrupt its smooth planes. The building is of straight warehouse construction. The interior at any point reveals a great sweep of open space divided into broad avenues marked off by the ranks of high, slender columns. The extraordinarily wide bays and the unusual story height of 16 feet combine with the slender wrought-iron columns to make this dramatic impression of open and airy spaciousness. No other department store can quite match the Sears Roebuck in this respect. Typical of warehouse construction, the plan is a closed rectangle up to the sixth story. Above this level there is a shallow indentation one bay deep along the alley which flanks the rear elevation.

The importance of the Sears Roebuck Store lies in its formal excellence. The technical problems which it posed had been solved by Jenney in the Home Insurance Building. In the later structure the steel and wrought-iron skeleton became essentially and fully the means of architectonic expression. The interior frame furnishes the dominating accent of the elevation—the pattern of large, open rectangles into which the outer walls are divided. These panels or cells are filled with glass divided into either two

5. *Industrial Chicago*, I, 204.

or four large windows separated by thin wrought-iron mullions. The long west elevation is an organic revelation of the structural system behind it, just as the isolated buttresses of Gothic architecture serve as the primary element in its indissoluble unity of structure and form. In the Sears Roebuck Store the impartial equilibrium of the steel cage takes the place of the gravitational thrust of the bearing wall. The unbroken horizontal lines of the spandrels at every third story and the continuous vertical lines of the piers provide a superb revelation of the construction of steel and wrought-iron framing. The inappropriate details are reduced to a negligible point. Only the uneven rhythm of the wide and narrow piers (the latter of which are deliberately obscured) mars the harmony of the street elevations.

The Sears Roebuck Store was the work of a man of rare courage and imagination. In the language of *Industrial Chicago:* "It has been constructed with the same science and all the careful inspection and superintendence that would be used in the construction of a steel railway bridge of the first order. . . . Designed for space, light, ventilation, and security, the Leiter Building meets the object sought in every particular. . . . A giant structure . . . healthy to look at, lightsome and airy while substantial, was added to the great houses of a great city, . . . a commercial pile in a style undreamed of when Buonarotti erected the greatest temple of Christianity."[6] The union of science, techniques, and art in this structure still represents a synthesis which is healthy indeed in a confused and divided world. Yet Jenney, as his later buildings show, seems not to have realized the soundness of his own intuition.

THE CLIMAX OF JENNEY'S CAREER

Three large buildings designed by Jenney were completed in 1891, and all three stand today. The first and largest is the Fair Store, extending along the north side of Adams Street from State to Dearborn (Fig. 32). Construction began in 1890 and was completed in a year and a half. The Fair is considerably

6. *Ibid.*, p. 205.

greater in volume than the Sears Roebuck Store, being eleven stories high and having an area in plan of 55,000 square feet. It is of warehouse construction, like the earlier building, a closed rectangle in plan, a completely framed and fireproof structure. In spite of its great size (the total cost was $3,000,000) and its redundant profusion of decorative stonework, it is light and open in appearance. The elevations, though lacking clarity, are direct expressions of the light steel and wrought-iron cage which carries them (Fig. 33).

On the basis of a concrete foundation reinforced with rails, the frame of the Fair Store rises in a series of built-up box columns and deep I-beams. The flooring is laid on a subfloor of concrete which in turn is carried on fireproof tile arches. A tile envelope provides fireproofing for the columns. The construction was typical of the skyscraper with bolted frame (Fig. 34). The basic structural element of the Fair Store is revealed in the continuous piers and narrow spandrels of the street elevations, but the revelation is obscured by heavy-handed details. Two massive courses at the top of the fifth and sixth stories, respectively, divide the elevation into three parts in a clumsy 5-1-5 ratio. The rustication at the sixth story and the huge pier capitals at the fifth and eleventh detract still further from the validity of the design. The windows, as in all of Jenney's buildings, are relatively small as a result of the division of the bay into three parts separated by slender mullions. These are so thin, however, that the total area of glass is very large.

The Manhattan Building, at 431 South Dearborn Street, was completed in 1891 (Figs. 35, 36, and 37). The frame of this structure is carried on spread footings of concrete reinforced with rails. The unit load transmitted by the footing is 3,000 pounds per square foot. The exterior facing of the front and rear elevations is gray granite up to the fifth story, pressed brick and terra cotta above. In form the building is unusual, indicating that additions were made after completion. Originally it consisted of a central mass twelve stories in height flanked by two nine-story wings. Four additional stories were added a few years after completion.

What immediately strikes the observer of the Manhattan Building is the variety of window openings in the Dearborn Street elevation. There are large uninterrupted areas of glass set flush at the base, conventional windows paired in the second and third stories, trapezoidal bay windows in the middle three bays above the third story, and bay windows forming triangular projections above rounded spandrels in the wings. Above the twelfth story standard openings are paired under arches, as they were in any number of Chicago buildings erected during the eighties. The tripling of the rhythm in the top story is a late relic of Richardson's treatment of the walls in the Marshall Field Wholesale Store. This curious mixture of sizes and types of window openings in the Manhattan is not a matter of caprice. Jenney sought to admit as much light as possible along a narrow, densely built street. Where the Manhattan rises above its neighbors, the windows sink back into the primary wall plane. The method of framing projecting windows, which were very common in the work of the Chicago school, was probably developed by Holabird and Roche for the Tacoma Building. The skeleton of the Unity Building shown in the illustration was typical (Fig. 38).

An important structural innovation characterizes the Manhattan Building. Jenney had to face the problem of dangerously overloading the party walls and footings of the two low buildings that originally flanked the Manhattan. He solved it by carrying the floors along the outer bays of the side elevations on cantilever beams fixed to columns located on a line well inside the line of the party walls. This method of cantilevering the floor slab beyond the outermost line of columns is necessary wherever the architect chooses to employ continuous or ribbon openings. The most extensive use of the device was made by Howe and Lescaze in the Philadelphia Savings Fund Building, constructed in 1932.

The most crisp and elegant treatment of the elevation in all of Jenney's designs appears in the Ludington Building, 1104 South Wabash Avenue, erected in 1891 (Fig. 39). Through its regularity and harmony and its slim piers and spandrels, the light and open and graceful façade which is possible with steel framing is given full expression. The disfiguring elements of earlier buildings—the capitals, the rustication, the stout piers, and the uneven rhythm of wide and narrow members—are here reduced to a minimum. The capricious playing with surface is still evident, as in the little classical pilasters which adorn the piers at the end and center bays, but they are hardly noticeable except when sunlight at a sharp angle picks them out. The base of the Ludington is unusually fine: the narrow piers and the huge windowpanes set flush show how far the interior frame can be exploited for architectonic effect.

The Morton Building, at 538 South Dearborn Street, marks the beginning of Jenney's decline as an original architect (Fig. 40). It was built in 1896; after it, in the remaining ten years of Jenney's career, he fell before the classical fashion which he himself helped to perpetuate. When a man of his reputation bowed so willingly before the fake imported taste that was displayed at the 1893 Fair, there was little to expect from any quarter. The Morton Building is a compromise between the new architecture of the Leiter buildings and the dead tradition that was paraded on the Midway. The classical details go far toward hiding the genuine commercial style which Jenney brought close to perfection in his organic expression of skeletal construction. It is instructive to compare the Morton Building with the cleanliness and honesty of Holabird's Pontiac Building (1895), a portion of which appears immediately to the left of it in the illustration (Fig. 40).

CHAPTER V

Burnham and Root

THE SECOND RAND MCNALLY BUILDING

JOHN WELLBORN ROOT had little time to master the architecture of steel framing before his death in 1891. A good part of the last few years of his life was devoted to the design and supervision of the Monadnock. The first commission of Burnham and Root in which the architects used complete skeletal construction was that for the second Rand McNally Building, the first structure to be supported on an all-steel frame. It was erected in 1889–90 on the block bounded by Adams, La Salle, Quincy, and Wells streets. It was demolished in 1911, and in the following year the present Rand McNally Building, designed by Holabird and Roche, was completed. The building was a huge rectangular prism ten stories in height which nearly filled the site bounded by the four streets. An interior court roofed by a skylight brought light to the inner portions of the floor area. Jenney's system of cantilever supports for carrying party walls was also used in the Rand McNally, in part to spare its lesser neighbors from the danger of excessive settlement.

For the most part the elevations of the Rand McNally were well articulated, expressing with little hesitancy the frame on which they were carried. The piers and spandrels were narrow and bounded unusually large areas of glass. But the whole treatment of the elevations was unnecessarily restless and involved. The arbitrary division of the façade into separate horizontal areas was carried to an extreme. The base was relatively straightforward. Above the first story ran a horizontal course marking it off from those above it. The piers at the second story had capitals. A second belt course separated the third and fourth stories, distinguished by heavy recessed spandrels. The fifth, sixth, and seventh stories constituted another division characterized by flat arches spanning the bays at the top of the seventh. The piers at this division were continuous, their width decreased, and the spandrels again recessed. The eighth and ninth stories were also separated from each other and from the rest of the structure by continuous belt courses. The tenth merged with the parapet that terminated the elevation.

This separation of the wall into horizontal areas differentiated by variations of detail was capricious and illogical. The skeleton is a perfectly regular cage which is uniform from top to bottom. Root's treatment was in no way required or suggested by internal functional arrangements. It is to his credit as an architect, however, that the details were completely subordinated to the dominant expression, which was in large outline unequivocal. The natural horizontality of the large office building—it is, after all, a vertical succession of uniform horizontal planes—is a perfectly valid basis for expression. But to secure such expression means that every story must be treated in the same way. Root accomplished this in the Montauk, where thin terra-cotta bands marked off each story. In spite of the continuity of piers in the Rand McNally, there is a general feeling of logical horizontality which helps to emphasize the neutrality of the framing.

THE GREAT NORTHERN HOTEL

The refinement of statement exhibited by the Monadnock was bound to appear in Root's handling of framed construction. It came with the Great Northern Hotel, which stood from 1891 to 1940 on the northeast corner of Dearborn Street and Jackson Boulevard (Fig. 41). As a hotel the Great Northern takes its place with the work of Theodore Starrett and Clinton J. Warren, the leaders of hotel design, by virtue of the application of new structural and formal ideas to a type of building other than the office block. In this respect it has an additional importance in the history of architecture. It was one of the magnificent achievements of the Chicago school. If it were standing today, it would still be one of the few hotels in the country to reveal a genuine architectural sophistication. As a matter of fact, except for the Chicago work of the 1890's, there was scarcely a hotel in the United States to compare with it until the completion of Skidmore, Owings and Merrill's Terrace Plaza in Cincinnati in 1948.

Burnham and Root had had little preparation for the Great Northern. They had received several commissions for apartment buildings, the best of which were the Argyle and the Pickwick, both completed about 1887. Theodore Starrett's Hyde Park Hotel probably provided the important precedent.[1] Aside from their having to deal with the many functional problems specifically associated with hotel design, the architects attacked the Great Northern in the same way that they approached the office block. As Harriet Monroe said, "It was planned as rigorously for space and light as an office building."[2] The many utilitarian features of the hotel followed the innovations made by Starrett and developed by Clinton Warren. We will take them up in the chapter dealing with the general subject of hotels and apartments.

The Great Northern was a fourteen-story structure supported on a steel and wrought-iron frame. Its exterior envelope was uniform in material, brick from top to bottom except for a small amount of terra-cotta trim. Interior fireproofing was the most extensive at the time of construction. The architects claimed that no fire originating in a room could spread beyond it or the suite of which it was a part. The street elevations of the building well expressed the nature and arrangement of interior facilities—a series of similar rooms or apartments along central corridors, each floor above the second planned like every other. A small portion of space on the lower floors was given to offices and stores; otherwise the volume was devoted entirely to rooms, lobbies, service facilities, and other characteristics of a residential building.

1. See chapter x, the section on "The Hyde Park Hotel."

2. *John Wellborn Root*, p. 151.

The unity, purity, and regularity of the Great Northern provided the source of its aesthetic excellence. The projecting bays in the walls were handled with a sure sense of relationship and function. On the Dearborn Street elevation the central bay projected in trapezoidal plan, as did the three projecting bays on Jackson Boulevard. The rest were rounded in plan. The corner over the entrance and the northwest corner were developed into cylindrical pavilions which extended beyond the main wall planes to an amount equal to that of the bay windows. The primary purpose was functional—to secure the maximum admission of light—but the general treatment indicates a formal interest in handling the big structure as a plastic-utilitarian object.

The only vestige of traditional ornament was at the parapet and the cornice above the thirteenth story. The flattened arches over the windows at the twelfth story and the tripling of the window rhythm at the fourteenth suggest the influence of Richardson. For the most part, however, the hotel was a great cage clothed in a thin envelope of brick, the openings marked by two large windows that filled each of the bays. The Great Northern was undoubtedly Root at his best. The technical and aesthetic principles of Chicago construction were here adapted to the requirements of a hotel building which revealed, simply but powerfully, the soundness of those principles.

THE ASHLAND BLOCK

The formal characteristics embodied in the Great Northern Hotel appeared, fortunately, in one building which stood until 1949. It was the Ashland Block, opened for occupancy early in 1892, at the northeast corner of Clark and Randolph streets (Figs. 42 and 43).[3] The original Corinthian cornice of the Ashland was removed and replaced by a plain parapet, which appears in the second illustration (Fig. 43). The parapet is grotesquely out of scale with the elements of the walls and consequently ruins the appearance of the building at the top. Aside from this clumsy alteration, however, the Ashland retained in

3. The Ashland was demolished in the fall of 1949 to make way for the new Union Bus Terminal.

comparison to its newer neighbors the unity and harmony and simple expressiveness which made it one of the proudest structures of the Chicago school.

In construction, materials, and general exterior design the Ashland was almost identical with the Great Northern Hotel. It was higher and more elongated in plan, but the over-all impression was much like that of the hotel building. Brick and terra-cotta facing formed the envelope of the steel and wrought-iron frame. Except for the semicircular arches which spanned the bays at the top of the third story and the triple openings of certain bays in the long elevation, the fenestration was close to that of the Great Northern. The wall at alternate bays projected in rounded outline, and the three street corners were developed into cylindrical pavilions. The ornamental details of the exterior were reduced to little more than the original cornice and the capitals of the piers at the third story. The horizontal division, effected by means of the separate treatment of the base and by the continuous courses at the seventh and fifteenth stories, was still present but reduced to an unobtrusive point.

Like Jenney, Root never opened the building wall to the extent possible with framed construction. The Ashland contained the greatest area of glass to be found in any of his buildings, yet the conventional separate openings of the Montauk and the Monadnock remain the basic unit of fenestration. It remained for Holabird and Roche three years later to merge the windows into a continuous opening extending across the width of the entire bay. The pattern of openings in the wall of the Ashland is plainly derived from the form of the skeleton, but as an expression of the structural basis it lacks the clarity and vigor of Jenney's second Leiter Building. The simplicity, directness, and functionalism of Chicago construction predominate in the Ashland Building, and one sees in it, approaching maturity, the full aesthetic statement of new structural and utilitarian factors.

THE WOMAN'S TEMPLE AND THE MASONIC TEMPLE

Two of Root's last designs were excursions into the romantic. The Woman's Temple, commissioned by the Woman's Christian

Temperance Union, was a translation of Romanesque and French Gothic details into the vocabulary of commercial architecture (Fig. 44). The building, completed in 1891, stood at the southwest corner of La Salle and Monroe streets. In the hands of a lesser architect it would have been vulgar licentiousness. The two-story base of massive stone, the steeply pitched roof, the great arches at the ninth story, the deep reveals, the dormers and pinnacles, came straight from the handbooks, yet Root's skill and sense of harmony dominated them, and somehow out of these excessive details the real nature of the building emerged. It was florid stuff, arty and "feminine," but the central portion or "shaft" stood out, and it was here that structure guided and informed the outer expression. The important functional characteristic of the Woman's Temple was its H-plan, representing an admirable solution to the problem of admitting sufficient natural light into a deep building.

Harriet Monroe tells us that the richness and exuberance of the Temple grew in part from Root's answer to the suggestion that the building ought to express the aspirations of the earnest crusaders who commissioned it. Yet one wonders whether it really reflected the personality of Frances Willard and her sisters. The so-called "femininity" of the design may well have embodied the very thing that she and her cohorts fought against and ultimately triumphed over.

The Masonic Temple, on the northeast corner of State and Randolph streets, was the leading skyscraper in 1891 (Fig. 45). It was the highest building of its time—twenty-two stories if we go to the ridge line of the attic—and the owners boasted that it was the most expensive. It suffered the fate of much of Root's work when it was demolished in 1939. Above the sixteenth story the Masonic was a piece of extravagant traditionalism. The Venetian and Tudor windows, the steeply pitched roof, the dormers and decorated gables, were all pretentious and redundant, an orgiastic conclusion to the base-shaft-capital program. Between base and capital, however, the pressed brick and terracotta facing provided a simple cover for a clean and honest structure whose continuous piers imparted a strong vertical accent suggesting Sullivan's skyscraper style of the Wainwright and other buildings. The neutrality of the steel cage was partly preserved, however, in the wide openings of the grouped windows.

Root was not satisfied with the Masonic Temple, but at the same time he felt that he had given the problem its best aesthetic solution. Tallmadge said, "He strove here to achieve a 'commercial style' based on the Romanesque which might be generally accepted as a formula for the expression of the skyscraper."[4] Root had come much closer to it in the Monadnock and the Great Northern, but he was obviously searching through richness of detail for what to him was a greater emotional impact than these buildings could show. He hardly achieved it in the Masonic Temple. Forty years of empty traditionalism in skyscraper design show how far he had strayed from the right course, which began with the Montauk and reached its high point in the Ashland and the Monadnock. The Ashland and the Masonic once stood two blocks apart on Randolph Street (Fig. 46). It took American architects nearly two generations to recognize the immense superiority of the former.

4. Thomas E. Tallmadge, *Architecture in Old Chicago*, p. 204.

CHAPTER VI

D. H. Burnham and Company

THE MAJESTIC HOTEL

AFTER Root's death in 1891 Burnham continued the firm under his name alone. The chief designing architect of the office was Dwight Perkins, whose fame as a member of the Chicago school is based on his design of Carl Schurz High School, built in 1910. Whether the guiding spirit was Perkins' originality or Burnham's recollection of Root's principles is a difficult question to determine. For three years the work of D. H. Burnham and Company remained at the level Root had reached. After 1895, however, it reflected the steady and progressive degradation of everything he stood for.

The design in which Root's talent continued to live was that of the Majestic Hotel, constructed in 1893 at 29 West Quincy Street, where it still stands today (Fig. 47). Its site is immediately adjacent to the north portion of that once occupied by the Great Northern, the rear elevation of which appears in the illustration. The presence of the older hotel determined the fenestration and general exterior treatment of the Majestic. The sense of form correlation was strong in the Chicago architects, and it survived even after the old originality had disappeared.

The façade of the Majestic is an exact continuation of the elevation of the Great Northern. The bay windows and the size and spacing of openings in the newer structure are patterned directly after those of the older. The projecting horizontal courses are carried without interruption across both buildings. The one at the top of the thirteenth story, however, shows that the desire for continuity sometimes got the better of good sense.

Since the Majestic has three full stories and a roof garden above the thirteenth, the interruption at that point is illogical. The horizontal course is repeated at the top of the fifteenth story, where it has some meaning. For the most part the Majestic Hotel is even more unified and homogeneous than the Great Northern. Except at the sixteenth and seventeenth stories, the motive is uniform from end to end and from top to bottom. The façade is perfectly neutral, a simple array of openings neither markedly horizontal nor vertical. Most of them are arranged in bay windows for maximum light and air; all of them together express the pattern of the steel cage behind them.

THE RELIANCE BUILDING

The path which Burnham followed in the Majestic Hotel had been well explored and marked. But the Reliance is astonishing in its daring pursuit of Chicago principles to their logical ultimate. The designing architect was Charles B. Atwood, a member of Burnham's staff. One short step more, and he would have produced the transparent tower that the new Internationalists imagined in their projects of the early 1920's. The Reliance Building, at 32 North State Street, was constructed in two parts: the first four stories were completed in 1890, the remaining ten in 1895. Thus Root may very well have had a hand in its original design. It represents the architectural culmination of Burnham's career and the goal that the whole Chicago movement was consciously or unconsciously striving to reach (Fig. 48). For here the last vestige of a bearing element has disappeared from the elevations.

The structure has no piers or columns in the exterior envelope, which is simply a vertical succession of broad glass bands divided into large panes by extremely tenuous mullions. The strong horizontality of the elevations is a direct revelation of the internal structure, a series of parallel, horizontal slabs carried to the columns by light beams. Atwood and Burnham succeeded in developing, almost to its ultimate refinement, the dematerialized curtain wall and thus made the building a direct forerunner of the work of Le Corbusier and Mies van der Rohe. The walls of the

65. TRANSPORTATION BUILDING, WORLD'S FAIR, 1893 — ADLER AND SULLIVAN

The only original design of the Fair and for many years Sullivan's best-known work. (*Chicago Architectural Photographing Co.*)

66. TRANSPORTATION BUILDING, WORLD'S FAIR, 1893 — ADLER AND SULLIVAN

Detail of the "Golden Door." (*Chicago Architectural Photographing Co.*)

67. STOCK EXCHANGE BUILDING, 1893–94 ADLER AND SULLIVAN

30 North La Salle Street. The Stock Exchange was moved to the new Board of Trade Building when that structure was completed in 1929. (*Commercial Photographic Co.*)

68. GRAND CENTRAL STATION, 1889–90 S. S. BEMAN

Southwest corner of Harrison and Wells streets. (*Chicago Architectural Photographing Co.*)

69. GRAND CENTRAL STATION, 1889–90 — S. S. BEMAN

Interior of the train shed. (*Allen Lein.*)

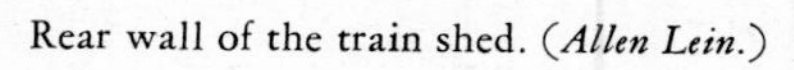

70. GRAND CENTRAL STATION, 1889–90 S. S. BEMAN

Rear wall of the train shed. (*Allen Lein.*)

71. GRAND CENTRAL STATION, 1889–90 S. S. Beman

Glass roof of the mail and baggage platform. (*Allen Lein.*)

72. STUDEBAKER BUILDING, 1895 S. S. BEMAN

Now the Brunswick Building, at 629 South Wabash Avenue. (*Commercial Photographic Co.*)

73. STUDEBAKER BUILDING, 1895 S. S. BEMAN

Main elevation. (*Commercial Photographic Co.*)

74. 200 WEST ADAMS STREET, 1888 BURLING AND WHITEHOUSE

(*Kaufmann & Fabry.*)

75. MALLERS WAREHOUSE, 1893 FLANDERS AND ZIMMERMAN

225 South Market Street. (*Chicago Architectural Photographing Co.*)

76. HYDE PARK HOTEL, 1887–88, 1891 — THEODORE STARRETT

Hyde Park Boulevard and Lake Park Avenue. (*Kaufmann & Fabry.*)

77. VIRGINIA HOTEL, 1889–90 CLINTON J. WARREN

Formerly the Leander McCormick Apartments, at the intersection of Ohio and Rush streets; demolished in 1929. (*Commercial Photographic Co.*)

78. METROPOLE HOTEL, 1891 — Clinton J. Warren

Michigan Avenue and Twenty-third Street. (*Commercial Photographic Co.*)

79. HOTEL MICHIGAN, 1891–92 — CLINTON J. WARREN

Formerly the Lexington Hotel, at the northeast corner of Michigan Avenue and Cermak Road. (*Commercial Photographic Co.*)

80. PLAZA HOTEL, 1892

CLINTON J. WARREN

1553 North Clark Street. (*Commercial Photographic Co.*)

Reliance form a thin skin stretched over the skeleton of the building and exhibiting a neutral tension in all directions. The appearance of a dematerialized skin or envelope arises not only from the extraordinary amount of glass but also from the fact that the glass is set nearly flush with the spandrels. The material of these narrow bands is glazed terra cotta, obviously without bearing capacity. The Reliance is the first building on which this material was used for exterior surfacing.

The windows of the Reliance form the most striking feature of the building. They represent the fullest development of the "Chicago window," in which a single large pane of glass fills the whole bay except for narrow movable sash at either end, immediately adjacent to the columns. The movable sash of the Reliance lies in the diagonal planes of the projecting windows and at the extreme edges of the openings in the parallel planes. "Ten years' experience," Giedion wrote, "lies behind the understanding treatment of the horizontally proportioned 'Chicago windows.' In earlier office buildings of the Chicago school the bow windows tend somewhat to be independent and isolated parts of the design. In the Reliance Building they project no more than they are required to in order to pick up light. They are wholly incorporated into the glass body of the building."[1]

The Reliance is not, like the Crystal Palace, a passing sensation produced for an exposition. It is a utilitarian structure commissioned as an office building, and it has been used as such for fifty-five years. Yet if any work of the nineteenth-century structural art anticipated the future, it is this one. The building, as Giedion states, is at once the triumph and the swan song of the Chicago school. In its grace and airiness, in the purity of its proportions and details, in the brilliant perfection of its transparent elevations, it stands today as an exciting tour de force in the structural art. Although it is outrageously disfigured by signs and by a "modernized" base, the essential beauty of this slim glass tower still reveals that it "has its place . . . as a witness to the best of the spirit of the nineteenth century."[2] Burnham

1. Sigfried Giedion, *Space, Time and Architecture*, p. 310.
2. *Ibid.*

fell into the confusion of eclecticism and conspicuous extravagance in his later years, but his reputation is secured by the Reliance Building.

THE DECLINE OF DANIEL BURNHAM

Burnham's designs after the Reliance show a progressive deterioration of both formal and functional quality. Most of his energy and originality immediately after the World's Fair were devoted to producing the Chicago Plan of 1895. Although this famous plan was geometric and formal rather than three-dimensional and organic, it revealed several important anticipations of twentieth-century town planning, especially in its disposition of major traffic arteries. Its most important feature was its exploitation of Chicago's natural setting, the shore line of Lake Michigan. Those portions of the plan embracing the lake-front development, the interior parks and parkways, and the through diagonal arteries were in large part realized. The magnificent achievement is Lake Shore Drive and its attendant system of parks, which rank with the great works of civic art in the past. The drive is the concrete embodiment of Burnham's brave dictum, "Make no little plans; they have no magic to stir men's minds."

But the history of Burnham the architect is a melancholy one. He knew the path of success, and he was willing to sacrifice much that had made Root and himself creative forces of the first rank. He was the victim first of the classicism which came from the East and which was flaunted so extravagantly at the Fair. The First National Bank Building, 1896, is a typical product. Except for the generous window area of its central portion and the structural characteristics, this building makes us feel that the Chicago school existed in vain. By the time the First National Bank was constructed many clients had come to believe that the school was an aberration, an old-fashioned thing that had no place in the new Gilded Age. This belief persisted until well into the 1930's. There was no truer prophecy than Sullivan's—"The damage wrought by the World's Fair will last for half a century from its date."[3]

3. Louis Sullivan, *The Autobiography of an Idea*, p. 325.

Burnham's next important commission, the Fisher Building, showed that in some respects he was still master of the structural art (Fig. 49). This building, which stands at 343 South Dearborn Street, was completed in 1897. It is in part the Reliance translated into Gothic terms. It is a high glass tower in which the structural expression has been obscured and disfigured by an incrustation of Gothic detail. But the fundamental lines and proportions, the open and airy grace, are there. To appreciate the Fisher Building, one has to see it in the late afternoon of a winter day. The semidarkness hides the detail; the lighting within transforms the wall into a glittering and transparent sheath crossed by thin horizontal and vertical lines. What the darkness covers became all-important in Cass Gilbert's Woolworth Tower, the most celebrated product of the Gothic trend which Burnham started.

The Railway Exchange Building, 1904, at the corner of Jackson and Michigan, was one of the last good designs that came from the office of Burnham and Company (Fig. 50). There is in it little dependence on historical styles and fairly consistent exploitation of Chicago construction. The extensive area of glass and the clean, sharp lines form a clear expression of steel framing. Above the course separating the thirteenth and fourteenth stories, however, the clarity is softened and obscured. The circular openings of the top story, like those of Sullivan's Wainwright Building, are mere arbitrary decoration and very poor as such. But the Railway Exchange stands at a great distance from the Reliance. Standard openings take the place of the Chicago windows of the older building, and the purity and bold transparency are gone. Burnham's Heyworth Building, constructed in 1905 at the southwest corner of Madison Street and Wabash Avenue, has much the same quality as the Railway Exchange but is somewhat superior to it in its greater unity and in the greater incisiveness of its articulation. But it was a farewell performance.

CHAPTER VII

Holabird and Roche

THE ARCHITECTS

IN THE long period of their practice, in the number and excellence of their buildings, in the consistency and uniformity of their designs, William Holabird and Martin Roche most completely represented the purpose and the achievement of the Chicago school. Individual buildings of Sullivan and Root are superior to anything they did, yet they discovered the simplest utilitarian and structural solutions to the problems of the big urban office block, and out of these solutions they developed what amounts to a standard form adaptable with minor variations to the conditions associated with the commercial structure in a crowded area. Holabird and Roche knew that they were on the right path, and they followed it with undeviating persistence. One of the consequences of this was that the principles of the Chicago school survived longer in their work than in that of any other architect.

William Holabird was born in American Union, New York, in 1854. Two years (1873–75) at the United States Military Academy provided him with all the formal education he received for his profession. He resigned from West Point over disciplinary action taken for aiding a sick friend—an act of charity which apparently involved some minor infraction of the rules. He moved to Chicago in 1875 and decided, with little previous thought, to become an architect. He acquired the best training he could have received anywhere by entering Jenney's office as a draftsman shortly after he arrived in the city. He formed the partnership of Simonds and Holabird in 1880, of Holabird,

Simonds and Roche in 1881. Two years later the firm became Holabird and Roche. Forty years of almost unbroken success followed the establishment of the office.

Martin Roche, who was born in Cleveland in 1855, had moved to Chicago with his parents in 1857. He entered Jenney's office in 1872, shortly after completing his public-school education. There is little material on his early career, but he probably remained with Jenney's firm until joining the partnership of Simonds and Holabird. His role in the office was that of codesigner specializing in interior work. The whole problem of design, however, was often divided equally between the two men until the number of commissions made necessary the organization of a large staff.

Holabird and Roche seemed to have approached the structural art in much the same objective and business-like way as Jenney did. Yet not only were they responsible for many structural and utilitarian innovations but they also succeeded in developing the clearest architectonic statement of steel framing up to Sullivan's Carson Pirie Scott Store, begun in 1899. The record of their commissions from 1883 to 1886 is meager, but their first great achievement, the Tacoma Building, undoubtedly marked a bold and unprecedented plunge into the new system of Chicago construction.

THE TACOMA BUILDING

The characteristic originality and imagination of the Chicago school entered vigorously into the design of the Tacoma Building (Fig. 51). Holabird and Roche received the commission in 1886; construction began the following year and was completed in 1889. The building stood on the northeast corner of La Salle and Madison streets until 1929, when it was demolished to make way for the present skyscraper known as Number One North La Salle. The later structure is hardly an improvement over the earlier. The Tacoma was the pride of the Chicago school in many ways, both structural and formal. Like the best work of Jenney, it represented the artistic expression of a systematic technical and scientific attack on the problems of construction and utility.

The technical innovations were numerous. The foundation, both in type and in construction, was at that time unique. Before excavation the builder made 50-foot test borings to determine the character of the subsoil. This preliminary investigation revealed the presence of several pockets filled with water and soft clay. These were pumped out or excavated and filled with concrete which was forced in under pressure. This method of stabilization is now used extensively, not only to provide proper support for the foundations of buildings, bridges, and dams, but also to fill soft spots in railway embankments. The foundation of the Tacoma, which was of framed construction except for the bearing walls of the inner elevations, was a floating raft of concrete, 20 inches thick, reinforced with I-beams. The footings along the north side of the building were used to support the party wall of the adjacent structure.

The skeleton of the Tacoma was of cast iron, wrought iron, and Bessemer steel. The spandrel beams and major floor beams were wrought iron, smaller beams were steel, and all columns, mullions, and lintels were cast iron. The frame was the first riveted skeleton and thus marked a great improvement in efficiency and speed of erection. The construction of the frame was unusual in one respect. The spandrel beams were anchored in the brick piers; deep wrought-iron girders spanned the bays from column to column, and the steel floor beams between girders carried the floor slab. The framing of each floor was thus treated as an independent horizontal truss. Even more unusual was the presence of two transverse interior brick walls, extending from foundation to roof and stiffened by diagonal rods, to carry part of the interior floor and roof load.

In its functional characteristics the Tacoma was perhaps the most advanced design of its time. The L-shaped plan made possible an outer exposure for every office. The floors rested on fireproof hollow-tile arches, and all columns were completely incased in fireproof tile. For the first time in a large commercial block all toilet and lavatory facilities were concentrated in a small area of two central floors, thus making it possible to centralize piping in a single service shaft. The bay windows of the

Tacoma were the product of careful study, by means of which the architects discovered the multiple value of projecting wall bays. The primary advantage was that they permitted the admission of light from three directions. Second, they were useful in summer in catching the breeze blowing parallel to the building elevation. Third, they broke up the direct wind load and thus reduced lateral pressure on the wall area. And, finally, they had a distinct aesthetic value in their reflection of light in several directions and in increasing the sense of lightness and openness evoked by the great area of glass disposed in several planes. The well-integrated handling of the projecting bay, along with the extensive transparent area, gave the Tacoma its most striking architectural quality. As we shall see, the architects employed this feature repeatedly in subsequent designs and always with great skill.

REFINEMENTS ON THE TACOMA THEME

The basic form of the Tacoma was repeated by Holabird and Roche in three framed buildings erected shortly after the completion of their first major work. The first was the Caxton Building, 508 South Dearborn Street, which was built in 1889–90 (Fig. 52). The bay-wide openings of the base, the projecting windows, the narrow openings grouped in the projections, and the brick and terra-cotta sheathing appeared in this twelve-story structure approximately as they did in its more famous predecessor. The rich ornament of the Tacoma's top story, however, gave way in the newer building to a very simple treatment in which the windows lie in the primary wall plane. The Caxton was wrecked in 1947 to make way for the Congress Expressway.

Holabird and Roche received the commission for the addition to the Monadnock, which was extended south along Dearborn to Van Buren Street in 1893 (Fig. 53). The extension is a framed structure, which appears in the very wide openings of the base and in the relatively large area of glass compared to that of the original portion. Again we see the narrow windows closely ranked in the projecting bays. Except for the heavy cornice, the arcade at the top story, and the sharp differentiation of base from main building mass, the extension of the Monadnock is in general proportions and disposition of major elements like Burnham and Root's north half. Outer exposure for all offices in the Monadnock was made possible by the narrow slablike form of the structure.

An unusual variation of the wall pattern first developed by Holabird and Roche appears in the Pontiac Building, erected in 1891 at 542 South Dearborn Street, where it still stands (Fig. 54). Instead of the usual projection whose width is limited to that of one bay, the architects here extended the wall outward in two wide projections, each spanning two bays. The projection at the center of each of the street elevations is conventional in form. No functional requirement dictated this treatment, which gives the illusion of increasing the glass area of the wall. The Pontiac, like the Caxton and the Monadnock addition, shows a failure to exploit the steel frame to full utilitarian and formal advantage. The individual windows are small, and between the groups of openings the envelope of the frame is solid throughout the height of the building. Before the construction of the Pontiac, however, Holabird and Roche had taken the decisive step in the architectonic revelation of steel framing.

THE MARQUETTE BUILDING

Later structures of Holabird and Roche are clearer and more refined than the Marquette, but it is the point of departure for all of them. It was erected in 1894 at 140 South Dearborn Street, where it still stands, fully occupied, one of the great office buildings of the Loop (Fig. 55). One may compare the Marquette with its neighbor on the left, also shown in the illustration, to see how far the architects of the 1920's had sunk below the level of the Chicago school. The precedent for the form of the Marquette was Jenney's second Leiter Building, the present Sears Roebuck Store. But Holabird and Roche turned away from the narrow openings and relatively heavy mullions of Jenney's buildings and their own earlier work to open the whole bay in a great horizontal sweep of glass. These "Chicago windows," as they came to be called, and the continuous piers standing out from the recessed spandrels became the distinguishing marks of nearly every office block designed by Holabird and Roche in the next fifteen years.

The plan of the Marquette is shaped approximately like a capital E. The long elevation on Dearborn Street corresponds to the vertical line of the letter; the two wings extending along Adams Street and the alley to the north are the upper and lower crossbars. A short extension in the center between the two wings is the tongue of the E. The offices are disposed in a single row along Dearborn Street and in double rows along the two wings. Thus every office has a maximum exposure to natural light. The middle extension, relatively the darkest part of the building, is the elevator hall around which the elevators are grouped in a spreading U. It is a perfectly functional arrangement which typifies the direct and practical approach of the Chicago architects to the utilitarian requirements of the office block.

The street elevations of the Marquette set it off from all its predecessors. The windows are long rectangular openings extending throughout the width of the bays. Most of them are divided into four parts separated by mullions so thin as to be almost unnoticeable. The sash in the two center divisions is fixed; that at the ends is movable. The true Chicago window appears in the base or first two stories. Here a very long, horizontally disposed, single pane of glass is flanked at either side by narrow sliding sash. This treatment of the windows not only allowed the maximum admission of light and the necessary quantity of outdoor air, but it also made possible the full and uninhibited expression of steel framing. The general appearance of the Marquette is that of a pattern of large uninterrupted areas of glass set in narrow frames of piers and spandrels. The wall is a nearly uniform array of rectangular cells precisely duplicating the steel cage which they cover. Deep reveals and unusually fine proportions give the Marquette an incisive and dramatic quality which raises it to the level of superior architecture in any style.

There are architectonic defects in the Marquette, lingering

elements of traditionalism which often appeared in the best Chicago work when the architects were striving for a monumental effect. The most obvious, perhaps, is the arbitrary horizontal division of the elevation into base, shaft, and capital: the two stories at the base and at the top, respectively, are sharply set off from the twelve intermediate stories. This decorative treatment denies the structural and functional unity of the building. A further denial exists in the enlarged width of the piers and the rustication of the stone envelope at the corner bays. The base and top, together with the corner bays, thus appear to inclose the entire façade in a massive stone frame devoid of any logical connection with the structural system of the building. This same treatment originally existed on the Adams Street elevation, but the later addition of the west bay (1905) takes away the symmetry and causes the decorative stonework to appear even more irrational.

But the virtues of the Marquette are so fine and so many that one would hardly want to make an issue out of its superficial defects. The whole quality of the structure is impressive: the openings are perfectly scaled and proportioned; the wide, smooth expanse of glass transforms the huge elevations into graceful patterns of light; and the deep reveals accent the steel cage on which the walls are carried. The Marquette is a striking integration of technical necessities with their aesthetic statement.

THE ACHIEVEMENT OF A STABLE FORM

The subsequent work of Holabird and Roche in the last decade of the nineteenth century reveals, with one exception, a systematic refinement and clarification of the fundamental form of the Marquette Building. The exception is interesting in several respects, however, and deserves separate mention before we proceed to more typical structures. It is the Old Colony Building, an unusual but arresting combination of elements developed by its own architects and by others who preceded them (Figs. 56 and 57). The Old Colony was erected in 1894 at 407 South Dearborn Street, one door removed from Jenney's Manhattan Building, which appears at the right edge of both illustrations.

The standard paired openings and the continuous piers of the Old Colony are features common to the buildings of Holabird and Roche. The cylindrical projections at the corners, forming perhaps the most striking characteristic of the building, are reminiscent of the pavilions which Root employed at the corners of the Great Northern Hotel. The continuous piers of the long elevation produce an unobtrusive vertical accent. This is reversed in the narrow north elevation, where the architects produced a sharp horizontality between the cylindrical embayments. One can easily see that they were attempting to contract the apparent width of the wide elevation and expand that of the narrow. The high slablike form of the Old Colony makes possible the outer exposure of all offices. The only disfiguring element of the building, otherwise a handsome and well-porportioned structure, is the ridiculous colonnade at the fourteenth and fifteenth stories.

After the Old Colony and the Pontiac, Holabird and Roche rapidly developed a standardized form for the office building based on the design of the Marquette. From their drafting tables came one building after another, each almost identical with its predecessor. A single general description serves to cover the fundamental characteristics of all of them. The street elevations are cellular walls of large rectangular openings, each filling the entire bay. The piers are almost invariably continuous, the spandrels generally recessed to the point where they are nearly flush with the openings. Piers and spandrels are always much narrower than those of the Marquette. Chicago windows are common, but the narrow grouped openings separated by extremely tenuous mullions sometimes appear. Uniformity from end to end and from base to top came to replace the decorative variations of the Marquette. This treatment of the elevation, as we have seen in the case of the Marquette, answered the functional requirements of light and air while at the same time honestly expressing the structural system of steel framing.

The original Champlain Building, constructed in 1894 at the northwest corner of State and Madison streets, was typical of the large office blocks. Its fifteen stories were a succession of

Chicago windows bounded by the terra-cotta sheathing of the slim piers and spandrels. The Champlain suffered the most outrageous premature demolition of all Chicago office buildings. It was razed in 1916—its twenty-second year—to make way for the Boston Store, whose owners recently went out of business and left the building vacant. In 1949 the Boston was renovated and turned into an office block. This building is a reasonably good example of the designs of Holabird and Roche except for the preposterous colonnade at the top two stories.

Especially refined examples of the later work of Holabird and Roche are the two little structures at 24 and 30 South Michigan Avenue, which form, with Sullivan's design immediately north of them, the three buildings of the Gage group (Figs. 58 and 59). Construction of the first two was completed in 1898. The "modern" store fronts, appearing in the second illustration, spoil the fine sweep of glass which originally characterized the base of these buildings. Their frank clarity and exactitude are the product of uniformity of treatment, the absence of decorative detail, and the presence of large Chicago windows in the small façades.

A return to the paired standard openings recessed from the continuous piers marks the Williams Building, 1898, at 205 West Monroe Street (Fig. 60). The sharp angle of the photograph obscures the unusually light and open quality of the façade. A structure very much like the Williams was erected at 320 South Franklin Street in 1898, but it has been demolished. The former Cable Building (now Hoops), at the southeast corner of Wabash Avenue and Jackson Boulevard, was completed in 1899 (Fig. 61). Here Chicago windows were replaced by groups of four narrow openings of sliding sash separated by thin mullions. A suggestion of the Marquette appears in the way the heavy corner piers and the cornice enframe the otherwise light and graceful elevations. The unusual feature of the Cable Building is the continuous opening at the first and second stories. The former McClurg Building (now Crown), at 218 South Wabash Avenue, was erected in 1899–1900 (Fig. 62). This is an extraordinary example of how far Chicago architects could go in reducing the façade of a framed structure to mere lines. The presence of fluting on the knife-edged piers heightens the tenuousness of these members.

When we examine the work of Holabird and Roche in the twentieth century, we shall see a continuation of the same characteristics we have noted here. The uniformity of their work is so striking that with a little familiarity one can pick out their designs all over the Loop and adjacent blocks. Some critics have complained that their work after the Marquette reveals a monotonous repetition of a hackneyed formula. Those who do, however, fail to appreciate the value of a true standard in architecture—that is, a basic norm or type exactly developed to fit a particular set of conditions and repeated wherever those conditions exist. This is a case where a formula represents an adequate generalization, deviations from which would be mere caprice or illogicality. The work of Holabird and Roche is not sterile repetition; it is the achievement of a stable form. It is to their credit that they rendered unnecessary a fresh act of imagination with every commission. Imagination and individual expression are vital, but let us remember with Whitehead that ultimately "civilization advances by extending the number of important operations which we can perform without thinking about them."[1]

1. Alfred North Whitehead, *Introduction to Mathematics* (New York: Oxford University Press, 1948), p. 42.

CHAPTER VIII

Adler and Sullivan

THE GARRICK THEATER BUILDING

ADLER and Sullivan's first commission involving the complete use of steel and iron framing was the Wainwright Building in St. Louis, built in 1890–91.[1] This structure represents Sullivan's first deliberate attempt to create a special form appropriate to the multistory office block. Here he employed his system of closely ranked piers to give the main elevations a pronounced vertical effect. In order to secure this sharp verticality, he placed false piers between the real piers or envelopes of the outer columns. The result is a building which exhibits a pleasing textural quality, but its form is the produrt of the artist's personal treatment of the wall as a plastic thing. The major progress of the Chicago school was in the direction of an articulated wall which expresses the structural facts of interior framing. The classic statement of this intention is Sullivan's Carson Pirie Scott Store, but many experiments in form stood between the skyscraper verticalism of the Wainwright and the structural articulation of the Carson store.

The building in Chicago which stands closest in outward form to the Wainwright is the old Schiller Building, now the Garrick Theater, constructed in 1891–92 at 64 West Randolph Street (Fig. 2). Once again it is Adler's engineering skill which arrests our attention as much as does Sullivan's artistry. The familiar raft foundation of concrete is laid, in the case of the

1. On Sullivan's attitude toward the architectural problem of the tall building see his "The Tall Office Building Artistically Considered," *Lippincott's Magazine*, LVII (March, 1896), 403. The most thorough analysis of the Wainwright Building is in Hugh Morrison, *Louis Sullivan*, pp. 144–56.

Garrick Theater Building, on a huge grillwork of oak timbers supported in turn by eight hundred 50-foot timber piles driven to refusal in hard-pan clay. The piling represents a forward step toward the true caisson foundation which Adler developed for the Stock Exchange Building in 1893. The periphery of the raft under the Garrick Theater is cantilevered beyond the grillwork to support the party walls of adjacent buildings without overloading their footings.

Above the foundations, on a wrought-iron and steel frame, rises a combination theater and office building which is perhaps Sullivan's most unusual design. The plan is shaped like a capital T with a short crossbar. The central tower of the Garrick Theater, seventeen stories high, is flanked by two nine-story wings. In back of the tower, corresponding to the stem of the T, is a fourteen-story wing. By means of this plan Sullivan was able to provide at least one outdoor exposure for every office. The entire ground floor of the Garrick Theater Building is taken up by the entrance lobby and the theater. The upper gallery extends to the fifth floor. The offices occupy the floors above the theater, the flanking wings on Randolph Street, and a narrow space above the lobby, between the theater and the street. The Garrick Theater was originally built for a German theatrical society and once contained clubrooms and dining facilities. The theater proper, now devoted entirely to movies, is another good example of the workmanship and artistry that went into the Auditorium. The ceiling is a series of expanding elliptical vaults extending from the proscenium to the rear wall. Vision is unobstructed; acoustics are near-perfect; scale and spatial relationships are exactly calculated to give a sense of intimacy while preserving the necessary spaciousness of a large theater. The Garrick is in many respects the best movie theater in Chicago.

The central and commanding feature of the Garrick Theater Building is the tower. This remarkable example of Sullivan's restless individualism stems in part from the Auditorium. The walls are a series of narrow piers extending to the sixteenth story, where they are joined by arches. Their slender height, however, indicates that Sullivan's precedent was in greater part the Wainwright Building, without the earlier structure's false piers. Sullivan's intention in the Garrick Theater was to make of it "the proud and soaring thing" which he thought the tall building ought to be. He does everything to strengthen the upward sweep—it is "cast in one jet," as he describes it. It is a superbly integrated composition, treated with a delicacy and finish that seem strangely out of place among the structures of Jenney and Holabird and even Root at his most ornamental.

The details of the Garrick Theater Building are highly questionable for a work of large-scale commercial architecture, although one might argue that they are becoming to a theater. A richly ornamented arcade extends across the entire façade at the second story. An overhanging roof slab or block cornice, incrusted with foliate ornament, formerly topped the upward motion of the central shaft. The cornice was replaced by a parapet in 1948. Scale is perfectly worked out for equal emphasis of the ornamentation at base and roof line. The total impression is one of elongated height circumscribed by an exuberant architectural lyricism, the whole complex belying the fundamental structural nature of the building. The Garrick Theater is an almost exotic exhibition of virtuosity without logic and with little organic quality. As a matter of fact, it is much less organic and hence less promising than its former neighbor, Sullivan's Borden Block (Fig. 2).

EXPERIMENTS IN FORM

The approach to the Gage Building and the Carson Pirie Scott Store was extremely irregular. There was, first of all, a brief return to masonry construction and an attempt to refine it beyond the severity of the Monadnock itself. This was the warehouse of the Chicago Cold Storage Exchange, completed in 1891 on West Lake Street near the Chicago River. The two blocks of the warehouse were nearly windowless above the second story, great solid masses covering an area of over 59,000 square feet. Sullivan deliberately and with considerable success set out to reduce architectural expression to the fundamental elements of volume and plane. It was a study in texture and geometric purism. After an investment of $1,500,000 and a useful life of eleven

81. CONGRESS HOTEL, 1893, 1902, 1907 — CLINTON J. WARREN, HOLABIRD AND ROCHE

504–20 South Michigan Avenue (at Congress Street). The north block (*right*), the work of C. J. Warren, was completed in 1893; the south block (*left*), designed by Holabird and Roche, was built in two sections, the first four bays completed in 1902, the remainder in 1907. (*Commercial Photographic Co.*)

82. LAKOTA HOTEL, 1893

Southeast corner of Michigan Avenue and Thirtieth Street. (*Commercial Photographic Co.*)

83. BREWSTER APARTMENTS, 1893 R. H. TURNOCK

Northwest corner of Diversey Parkway and Pine Grove Avenue. (*Kaufmann & Fabry.*)

84. CARSON PIRIE SCOTT STORE, 1899, 1903–4, 1906 LOUIS SULLIVAN

Originally the Schlesinger and Mayer Store, at the southeast corner of Madison and State streets. This building is the ultimate triumph of the Chicago school and by far its most famous creation. It is perfectly fitting that it stands on what has been traditionally known as the "world's busiest corner." (*Chicago Architectural Photographing Co.*)

85. CARSON PIRIE SCOTT STORE, 1899, 1903–4, 1906 — Louis Sullivan

Detail of the corner pavilion and the west elevation, showing the parapet which replaced the cornice in 1948. (*C. W. Condit.*)

86. CARSON PIRIE SCOTT STORE, 1899, 1903–4, 1906

LOUIS SULLIVAN

Detail of the west elevation. (*C. W. Condit.*)

87. CHAMPLAIN BUILDING, 1903 — HOLABIRD AND ROCHE

Originally the Powers Building, at the northeast corner of Monroe Street and Wabash Avenue. (*Commercial Photographic Co.*)

88. BAILEY BUILDING, 1898, 1903 — HOLABIRD AND ROCHE, NIMMONS AND FELLOWS

529 South Franklin Street. (*Kaufmann & Fabry.*)

89. 325 WEST JACKSON BOULEVARD, 1904, 1911 — HOLABIRD AND ROCHE

(*Commercial Photographic Co.*)

90. BORN BUILDING, 1908, 1927 HOLABIRD AND ROCHE, A. S. ALSCHULER

540 South Wells Street. (*Chicago Architectural Photographing Co.*)

91. CHICAGO BUILDING, 1904 — HOLABIRD AND ROCHE

Southwest corner of State and Madison streets. (*Chicago Architectural Photographing Co.*)

92. REPUBLIC BUILDING, 1905, 1909 HOLABIRD AND ROCHE

209 South State Street. (*Chicago Architectural Photographing Co.*)

93. MANDEL BROTHERS ANNEX, 1906 HOLABIRD AND ROCHE

Northwest corner of Wabash Avenue and Madison Street. (*Chicago Architectural Photographing Co.*)

94. BROOKS BUILDING, 1909–10 HOLABIRD AND ROCHE

223 West Jackson Boulevard. (*Chicago Architectural Photographing Co.*)

95. NEPEENAUK BUILDING, 1901–2 RICHARD E. SCHMIDT

Formerly the Chapin and Gore Building, at 63 East Adams Street. (*Chicago Architectural Photographing Co.*)

96. MONTGOMERY WARD WAREHOUSE, 1906–8 — Schmidt, Garden and Martin

North side of West Chicago Avenue at the River. (*Montgomery Ward & Co.*)

years, the warehouses were demolished. The cost of progress has seldom been higher.

The little Victoria Hotel in Chicago Heights, built in 1892–93, could hardly be classed with the work of the Chicago school, but its originality of form bears the clear stamp of Sullivan and also indicates the presence of Frank Lloyd Wright, who became Adler and Sullivan's chief designing assistant in 1893 (Fig. 63).[2] The over-all design of the Victoria is Sullivan's, but the surface ornament at the third story and at the top of the tower is very likely Wright's. It is a regular geometric pattern which anticipates the tile ornament in the second-story elevations of the Coonley house. The Victoria represents a romantic conception, almost pastoral, perhaps, befitting the rural nature of Chicago Heights before the metropolitan area engulfed it.

The architecture of steel framing emerges with relative clarity in the Meyer Building, constructed in 1893 at the southwest corner of Franklin and Van Buren streets (Fig. 64). It still stands unchanged except for the replacement of the original cornice by a parapet. The Meyer, a wholesale store building, is of brick facing devoid of ornament except for the narrow terracotta bands crossing the piers at the lintel and sill lines. The structure reveals, however, that Adler's sense of function was once more sacrificed to Sullivan's sense of form. He here reversed the accent of the tall Garrick Theater Building by sharply emphasizing the horizontality of the long, low block. The uninterrupted continuity of the spandrels is a product of their unnecessary width and the ornamental bands across the piers. The exterior masonry envelope is heavy enough to suggest masonry construction, but the horizontality, the narrow piers, and the large glass area of the base belong to the architecture of steel framing.

Sullivan's excursion into the ephemeral architecture of expositions was his Transportation Building at the World's Fair of 1893 (Fig. 65). This structure was for forty years the most famous of Sullivan's designs and the one which was generally felt to be the most representative of his peculiar genius. It hardly

2. Wright entered the office in 1887 and remained until 1893.

stands on a level with many of his designs for permanent structures, but it is an honest and functional example of the architecture of temporary exhibition halls.

With the cornice height and the rhythm of the piers fixed by the architectural board of the Fair, Sullivan turned out the only fresh, original, and straightforward building on the site. He gave a frank statement of the temporary materials of which the structure was built: surfaces are perfectly flat, the profile sharp and rectangular, and the structural elements are reduced to a series of piers supporting an arcade without moldings or imitation stonework of any kind. The bright colors of red, orange, and yellow and the brilliant decoration of the celebrated "Golden Door" (Fig. 66) gave the Transportation Building a liveliness and gaiety that the double faking of the other structures lacked completely. The Golden Door was the most striking example of Sullivan's capacity for rich and intricate detail subordinated to great architectural simplicity. It was for this detail, more than anything else, that he received the medal of the Société des Arts Décoratifs. The architectural independence of the Transportation Building was consistent with Sullivan's estimate of the Fair's achievement: "The damage wrought by the World's Fair will last for half a century from its date, if not longer."[3]

THE STOCK EXCHANGE BUILDING

Of all the commissions of Adler and Sullivan or of Sullivan alone up to the Carson Pirie Scott Store, the one that enters most fully into the main stream of the Chicago school is the original Stock Exchange Building, now known by its address, 30 North La Salle Street (Fig. 67). The Stock Exchange was designed in 1893, while Wright was still with the firm, and constructed in 1894. It was the home of the Exchange until the present Board of Trade Building was completed in 1929. Now given over entirely to offices, it has remained one of the most popular buildings in the Loop. Its rental record is extremely good: even during the depression of the 1930's it was 95 per cent occupied. In both structure and form the Stock Exchange Building reflects

3. *The Autobiography of an Idea*, p. 325.

the same fertility of imagination that Adler and Sullivan revealed in the Auditorium, after which the Stock Exchange was their largest commission.

The building is of standard fireproof steel-framed construction. It was for the foundation that Adler developed another of his many innovations. Over most of the building area the foundation rests on timber piles driven to bedrock 75 feet below grade level. The footings of the west line of columns, however, rest on massive concrete piers which also extend to bedrock. The concrete was poured in watertight drums which served as a form and as protection against seepage under pressure of the ground water. Thus on the west wall the Stock Exchange rests on the first true caisson foundation for buildings. The idea came originally from William Sooy Smith, who acted as engineering consultant for the Stock Exchange, but it was Adler who translated it into practice. The decision to use the caisson foundation was made in order that the presses of the *Chicago Herald*, whose building was formerly adjacent on the west side, would not be damaged by the blows of the pile-driver. Again a special problem gave rise to a great forward step in the progress of structural techniques. By means of the caisson foundation Adler ended once and for all the hitherto discouraging problem of excessive settlement.

The exterior form of the Stock Exchange is a reasonably organic outgrowth of steel framing without being a direct expression of it. Sullivan abandoned the plastic surface texture of the Wainwright and the Garrick Theater and treated the wall as a dematerialized plane. The general impression which the building makes is that of a great glass box poised lightly on the arcade of the third story. On the main portion of the street elevations, between the three-story base and the top story, Sullivan scrupulously avoided the use of ornament and refrained from either a vertical or a horizontal emphasis. Throughout its major area the wall becomes a thin curtain drawn in neutral tension over the projecting bay windows and the flat areas between. The quality of a skinlike envelope is heightened by the shallow reveals and by the absence of continuous courses or bands, the molding around the windows forming closed rectangles.

But the ambiguity so common in Sullivan's designs appears even in the advanced treatment of the Stock Exchange Building. It is the tension between the personal expression of the artist's individualistic temperament and the more impersonal statement of the structure and function of the building. The conflict appears first in the fenestration of the Stock Exchange. The narrow windows of the projecting bays stand independent of the large Chicago windows with their horizontal orientation. The two separate window sizes break up the elevations into numerous facets of glass which are not unified into a coherent pattern. Again we find the arbitrary horizontal division. The base, extending to the top of the third story, is topped by semicircular arches and enframed in an ornamental band of terra cotta. And the wall at the thirteenth story is recessed behind a narrow colonnade. Moreover, the base is too high in proportion to the total height of the building. Sullivan's originality and proud individualism are emphatically displayed. They point more clearly in the right direction than they do in previous designs, but the union of the Chicago style with his personal artistry was yet to come.

The Stock Exchange Building was Sullivan's last big commission until 1899, six years after it left the drawing boards. The panic and subsequent depression of 1893 stopped building once more and thus hit the architects hard. To Adler the situation looked dark enough to question the risk of hanging on. When Richard Crane in 1895 offered him the position of consulting architect and general sales manager of the Crane Elevator Company, he accepted. But the aggressive temperaments of the two men were antipathetic, and the contract was terminated six months after its acceptance. Adler wanted to reform the partnership, but Sullivan felt that he had deserted the firm in a trying period and refused. The two men founded separate practices in 1895. Adler died in 1900, his name having already disappeared from the roll of the great Chicago architects. The refusal to reform the partnership was Sullivan's greatest mistake.

Adler, the cool and practical man, was the necessary balance to Sullivan's reckless pride.

The number of his commissions declined rapidly. He received only two more in Chicago before the dismal period from 1900 to his death in 1924, during which his business as an architect virtually disappeared. One was for the Gage Building, which involved only a façade; the other was for the Carson Pirie Scott Store, which had actually been offered to the firm before Adler departed. The latter was Sullivan's swan song and the summation of the Chicago school's mature achievement.

THE GAGE BUILDING

We have already discussed the two earlier buildings of the Gage group in connection with Holabird and Roche. They received the commission for all three, at 18, 24, and 30 South Michigan Avenue, in 1898. The treatment of the façade of No. 18 was intrusted to Sullivan, and the entire structure was completed in 1899 (Figs. 58 and 59). Originally it was eight stories in height, but four more were added in 1902. Holabird and Roche drew the plans for the addition but followed Sullivan's design in every detail.

The little Gage Building is important in two respects. It was the first structure designed by Sullivan to take its form throughout the façade from the steel frame which supports it. In comparison to the frank clarity of Holabird's two buildings adjacent to it, Sullivan's personal idiom stands out. Yet the expression is disciplined by the articulation appropriate to framed construction and by a sound functional approach to the special problem of lighting involved here. Across the top of each window group, which extends over the entire width of the bay, Sullivan placed a 4-foot-high band of translucent glass to reduce and diffuse the glare of direct sunlight. Since the building was originally designed for a millinery establishment, this diffusion of light was necessary for close needlework. Sullivan was criticized for this supposedly aesthetic innovation, but actually his solution was superior to the full transparent openings of Holabird and Roche's buildings.

In the Gage Building extremely tenuous piers, narrow spandrels, flat glass base, and large openings set flush in the wall plane give a better sense of lightness and structural honesty than do any of Sullivan's previous designs. The cage of the steel skeleton is plainly but delicately expressed in the façade of the building. The emphasis on thin horizontal and vertical elements and the resolution of these elements into a finely proportioned composition give the little structure a firm but subtle quality which is superior, as architectural poetry, to the vigor and directness of Holabird's buildings. But Sullivan's lavish ornament is again redundant, especially in the foliation spreading out from the top of the continuous piers. The next step which he took, to the Carson Pirie Scott Store, has a perfectly logical starting point in the combination of Holabird and Roche's imposing simplicity and his own mature understanding of the quality of fine architecture.

CHAPTER IX

In the Wake of the Pioneers

GRAND CENTRAL STATION AND THE STUDEBAKER BUILDING

SEVERAL architects whose work lacks the consistency and uniformly high level of that of the leaders nevertheless made important contributions to the total achievement of the Chicago school. Foremost among them, perhaps, was Solon S. Beman, a successful architect who received a considerable number of large commissions not only in Chicago but also in Milwaukee, Omaha, and Cincinnati. He was born in Brooklyn, New York, in 1853. After studying architecture in New York for eight years under Richard Upjohn, he came to Chicago in 1879. He enjoyed almost immediate prosperity, having designed during the eighties the Pullman Building at Michigan Avenue and Adams Street, the factories and company houses of the Pullman Company at Kensington on the Far South Side of Chicago, and the original buildings of the Procter and Gamble Company at Ivorydale in Cincinnati. Grand Central Station remains the most significant of his designs and one of the least publicized of the important Chicago structures.

Grand Central Station was built in 1889–90 at the southwest corner of Harrison and Wells streets for the Wisconsin Central Railway, now a subsidiary of the Soo Line (Fig. 68). The structure was later acquired by the Baltimore and Ohio Chicago Terminal, which is now the proprietary company, the Soo Line, Chesapeake and Ohio, and Chicago Great Western being the tenants. By the standards of the big-city terminal Grand Central is relatively small. It handles only twenty-five trains a day, the majority being operated by the Baltimore and Ohio, and includes only six tracks for passengers and three for mail and express. As in the case of all old terminals, platform canopies have been built beyond the limits of the train shed to accommodate trains of fifteen or sixteen cars.

The station building is not particularly important to the historian of the Chicago school. It is of masonry construction resting on concrete foundations supported in turn by 50-foot piles extending to hard-pan clay underlying the soft clay and mud of the topsoil. The clock tower at the corner, 222 feet high, was built first to avoid unequal settlement. The architectural treatment of the exterior represents a clean and handsome adaptation of Norman style with the emphasis on smooth planes and simple geometric masses. The main floor, which contains the waiting room, ticket offices, and toilet and dining facilities, is spacious and unusually warm and inviting. The interior cast-iron columns are covered with fireproof tile and imitation Mexican onyx, other wall surfaces being finished in brown Tennessee marble. The functional and aesthetic superiority of the building to others of its type is immediately apparent, especially if one compares it with such of its contemporaries as the Illinois Central Station or Dearborn Station prior to the modernization of the interior in 1946.

The feature which distinguishes Grand Central Station as a work of structural art is the glass-and-iron construction of the train shed, concourse, and taxi rotunda. The train shed, of the balloon type, has a span of 156 feet, a height of 78 feet, and an over-all length of 555 feet (Fig. 69). It was the largest shed of its kind except for the original Grand Central Terminal in New York, constructed in 1871. In construction and appearance it is one of the finest American counterparts of the great sheds of Barlow and Brunel in London.[1] The vault itself is corrugated

1. The whole subject of nineteenth-century train-shed construction deserves thorough investigation, which it has not received up to this time. The balloon shed provided the precedent in part for modern methods of spanning large areas by means of steel or concrete shells with no intermediate supports. Few examples of the balloon shed remain today, most of them having been replaced by platform canopies or continuous roofs supported by columns. The largest single-span shed still in existence is that of St. Louis Union Station.

sheet metal supported on a series of parallel wrought-iron arch trusses of semicircular form. The spring line of the arches is flush with the platform surface; thus the vault forms a perfect half-cylinder of circular section.

The train shed is terminated at the rear by a glass wall exactly conforming in shape to a right section of the vault (Fig. 70). The lightness and openness of this wall is partly the result of the very thin sash inclosing the panes of glass and partly of the open trusswork brackets and columns supporting it. It is a superb example of glass-and-iron construction, one of the nineteenth century's major contributions to the structural art. The warm light diffused throughout the rear portion of the train shed comes in good part from the glass curtain. Much of it, however, comes from the glass roof which spans the mail and baggage platform (Fig. 71). This roof is carried from the arches to the building wall by means of light horizontal trusses. The clean wall planes and fine brickwork, the weightless and translucent surfaces of glass, and the delicacy of the wrought-iron members combine to form one of the Chicago school's most beautiful and most nearly forgotten examples of the new architecture.

The expert handling of large glass areas appears again in Beman's Studebaker Building, now the Brunswick, constructed in 1895 at 629 South Wabash Avenue (Figs. 72 and 73). In this building, however, the exactitude and direct structuralism of Grand Central Station have been overlaid by capricious and romantic Gothic ornament typical of Beman's love for redundant and fantastic details. Aside from the ornament and the contraction of the center bay, the façade is a great open area of glass crossed by the thin lines of the molded piers and the narrow bands of the spandrels. The recent removal of the castellated parapet of the Studebaker improved the profile of the whole structure, but the massiveness of the new brick parapet is radically out of keeping with the bright transparency of the façade. The Chicago windows and the sharply articulated wall provide the fullest exploitation of steel framing that the Chicago school could show at the time.

200 WEST ADAMS STREET

The little-known office and wholesale building at the northwest corner of Adams and Wells streets, erected in 1888, was the work of Burling and Whitehouse. Edward Burling, the senior partner, was the second architect to establish an office in Chicago. He was born in Newburgh, New York, in 1819. He started his career as a carpenter and at an early age became a housebuilder in his native town. He came to Chicago in 1843, worked with several builders for a few years, then founded an independent business. He established an architectural practice in the early 1850's, when J. M. Van Osdel was the only architect in the city. He formed a partnership with Adler in 1871 but dissolved it to form another with Whitehouse in 1879.

Edward Burling had no technical training as an architect. In spite of this handicap, he was highly successful, having designed a considerable number of buildings important in the history of Chicago. With no exception they revealed the historical eclecticism of nineteenth-century architecture until the design of the building at 200 West Adams Street (Fig. 74). The east elevation of this structure, along Wells Street, is superior to the façade because, although no different in treatment, its greater length gives it greater uniformity. The building is chiefly interesting for the fact that it represents an adaptation of the Richardsonian idiom to the architecture of interior framing. The influence of Richardson appears in the fenestration of the top story and of the end bays and in the emphasis on extensive wall surfaces. It is original, however, in the absence of arches and in the rounding of the corners of the piers and at other places where surfaces intersect. Except for the end bays, the elevations are fairly good expressions of steel framing. The smooth planes and the general rectangularity indicate that the architects were striving for a sense of volume rather than mass. If Richardson had lived, his commercial architecture may very well have moved toward the expression of the 200 West Adams Building. A number of buildings in the Loop area, more refined in one detail or another, are very much like it. A similar form, though on a larger scale, appears in the office block constructed in 1912 at the northwest corner of Jackson Boulevard and Wells Street.

THE MALLERS WAREHOUSE

Edward Burling trained an architect who was in large measure responsible for one of the astonishing structures of the Chicago school. He was John J. Flanders, the only architect of the school who was a native of the city. He was born in Chicago in 1848. After a few years in Burling's office he established his own practice in 1874. He formed the partnership of Flanders and Zimmerman in the late eighties. Flanders had designed an office building for the Mallers Company in 1884. He and his partner received the commission for the warehouse and wholesale store of the same company in 1892.

The Mallers Warehouse, now known simply by its address, 225 South Market Street, was completed in 1893 (Fig. 75). With the exception of the Reliance Building, this warehouse represents the most nearly complete dematerialization of the wall that one can find before the work of Le Corbusier in the early 1930's. It is a glittering prism of glass, all the more brilliant because of its setting among the begrimed buildings of the Market Street wholesale area. The base is a smooth plane of glass set flush with the outer surfaces of the columns. Above it rises a succession of horizontal glass bands stretched over alternate flat and projecting bays. Simple brick spandrels separate the standard windows, closely ranked with their thin mullions along the wall plane. The absence of any ornament except at the entranceway makes the Mallers Warehouse the purest revelation of steel framing until one comes to the work of the so-called International school in Europe—the Bauhaus, the Van Nelle Tobacco Factory, the Swiss Dormitory, the Maison Clarté.

It is here that the geometric purism of contemporary architecture first appears in its most refined form. A short step separates this perfectly functional and unpretentious warehouse from the bright parade of glass that distinguishes Mies van der Rohe's new buildings for Illinois Institute of Technology (Fig. 108). In fifty-five years the new architecture has come full circle, from Chicago through France and Germany back to its native home.

CHAPTER X

Hotels and Apartments

THE Chicago school developed the modern office building. For this it now enjoys a world-wide reputation. Yet its equally original, unprecedented, and influential work in the creation of the contemporary hotel and apartment has gone largely unpublished. The foremost architects of this type of structure—Theodore Starrett and Clinton J. Warren—were virtually unknown until Sigfried Giedion rediscovered them in *Space, Time and Architecture*. Chicago builders first met and dealt directly with the problem of the multiple dwelling for a rapidly expanding urban population. The Fire and the headlong growth of the city made it necessary, just as these factors presented the challenge and the opportunity out of which grew the modern office block.

The apartment house and the hotel of the present day were almost contemporary in their growth with the new office building. As we saw in the case of the Great Northern Hotel, the principles of construction and form evolved by the Chicago architects were applied to the multiple dwelling with the same daring, imagination, and success. The modern flat, like the office building, was necessitated by population density and made possible by the elevator and the interior skeleton. The Chicago architects made a direct functional attack on the apartment house, and the form which they developed was again an organic technical-aesthetic synthesis. The homogeneity and uniformity exhibited by the apartments and hotels is even more striking than in the case of the office building. It is once more a matter of developing the most rational standard, the generalization without exceptions, and using it wherever conditions indicated its propriety.

The technical innovations made or perfected by the Chicago architects have now become so common that, like all the great basic inventions on which our lives depend, they have come to be regarded as natural things which always existed. The important structural features created by the Chicago school were, of course, the steel frame, hollow-tile fireproofing, and the opening of the wall into glass. Out of these came the three-way exposure of apartments, making possible continuous cross-ventilation and at least two exposures to sunlight. In the matter of interior facilities the Chicago architects developed the essential requisite of privacy, sound insulation. The innovations in plumbing were astonishing: hot and cold running water at all times, continuously circulating steam or hot-water heat, and the rational organization of plumbing facilities whereby the various supply and drain lines could be tapped into continuous mains forming separate circuits, one for each function. Electric lighting early became standard in the Chicago hotel and flat, as did electric call bells and telephone communication. Most important, perhaps, for the history of architectural form were the development of the movable partition to vary the size and number of rooms in a suite and the creation of built-in service furniture such as chests, sideboards, and wardrobe lockers. And, finally, in pursuit of their aim to free the resident of the last care of homeownership, the Chicago architects introduced the safe-deposit vault at the central desk.

It is impossible to track these many innovations to their points of origin. Often they appeared simultaneously in several buildings. In some cases they were the work of anonymous contractors or engineering consultants. It is entirely possible that Pullman's rapid development of the sleeping car offered as many suggestions to the hotel architect as did the office building. Precisely where the new architecture of hotels and apartments begins cannot be definitely established. The evolution away from traditionalism toward a new functionalism and a new organic expression occurred throughout the eighties. Some of the more significant of the early apartment buildings of masonry construction were the following: 3200 South Prairie Avenue, 1882, designed by Adler and Sullivan; the Geneva on Rush Street, 1884; the Lafayette on Dearborn Street, 1886–87; the Morton on Michigan Avenue at Eighteenth Street, 1888–89; and the Parker on Cottage Grove Avenue at Thirty-first Street, 1889. *Industrial Chicago* singles out Clinton Warren's Virginia Hotel, 1889–90, as the first structure in which simplicity and direct expression of function become the basis of architectonic form. The Hyde Park Hotel, however, predates it by two years, and it was probably the first building of its kind of framed construction.

THE HYDE PARK HOTEL

Theodore Starrett designed the Hyde Park, which stands at the intersection of Hyde Park Boulevard and Lake Park Avenue (Fig. 76). The main block of the building was constructed in 1887–88, the addition in 1891. Starrett was not an architect by profession but a structural engineer who had worked with Burnham and Root and who later associated himself with the George A. Fuller Company, builders of many of the structures we have mentioned here. It is very likely that the design of the hotel was the work of a staff assembled by Starrett and the Fuller Company to handle this particular commission, with Starrett as a designing supervisor. He took full advantage of the many structural and utilitarian innovations which were rapidly gaining acceptance in the large Chicago buildings of the time. The Hyde Park contains so many of the features common to the new hotel and apartment house that a description of it fits nearly all the similar structures which were growing up around it.

The main block of the Hyde Park is an open rectangle in plan, the inner rooms receiving light from an interior court. Both the original structure and the addition are of standard fireproof iron-framed construction. The exterior treatment plainly reveals the precedent for the Great Northern and many other hotels erected during the nineties and the early years of the twentieth century. Some of the details are unobtrusively Romanesque in character, but for the most part the architectonic effect of the building is determined by the extensive glass area, the grouped windows, and the smooth wall planes appropriate to the architecture of framed construction. The exterior finish is of pressed brick with brown sandstone trim. The rounded extension or pavilion at each corner became the distinguishing mark of Chicago hotels in the decade following the completion of the Hyde Park. It was used to provide for exceptionally spacious and well-lighted apartments at the corners. The repetition of the form on either side of the three center bays, however, is purely decorative. Originally a cantilevered wrought-iron balcony extended entirely around the main block of the Hyde Park, but it has since been reduced to short lengths at the end elevations and across the façade at the center. Short balconies on the façade extend up to the sixth floor.

The main entrance of the hotel opens into a lobby 100 feet long by 50 feet wide, surmounted by a vaulted glass-and-iron skylight open to the interior court. The walls and columns of the main floor are richly finished in marble wainscoting. The rest of the main floor is given over to the usual assortment of reception rooms, public and special dining-rooms, elevator bays, and other facilities. Of particular interest is the provision of a special inclosed area for small children and nurses. This necessary feature is conspicuously absent from many large apartment and hotel buildings of the present time.

The three hundred rooms of the main block are arranged in suites of two- and five-room apartments. Standard utilitarian facilities include electrically operated elevators, electric lighting, telephone service, electric call and return bells, and steam heat. Starrett carefully avoided the tunnel effect of corridors by making them unusually wide, airy, and well lighted. Fire escapes are located at the ends of every hallway. Wide windows open to the cool breezes of Lake Michigan, which was in 1891 much closer to Lake Park Avenue than it is now. The Hyde Park Hotel was the ultimate in luxury, comfort, and refinement when it was constructed. Its bold and forceful architectural treatment still places it far above the extravagant, tasteless, and badly designed hotels that form the accepted standard in most big cities.

THE WORK OF CLINTON J. WARREN

Without question the justly acknowledged leader of the architects of hotels and apartments was Clinton J. Warren. After founding his own practice in 1886, he rapidly developed a specialized knowledge of the work in which he secured pre-eminence. None of his early commissions as an independent designer showed the architectural vigor and originality of his hotels. His most important office building is the Unity, on Dearborn Street near Madison, erected in 1891. Its unusual characteristic is the complete cast-iron frame supporting its eighteen stories. But classical details and poor fenestration place it well below the level of contemporary office blocks and his own apartment buildings.

Warren's first large commission for a multiple dwelling was the Virginia Hotel, originally known as the Leander McCormick Apartments, erected in 1889–90 at the intersection of Ohio and Rush streets (Fig. 77). It was demolished about 1929. "All the modern improvements are found in this building," wrote the authors of *Industrial Chicago*.[1] And, more, it revealed the most advanced architectural treatment of its time. It was a ten-story and basement steel-framed structure sheathed in brown sandstone at the first story and dark-red pressed brick above. The hotel was divided into three parallel blocks separated by two 16-foot courts closed at the north end and open at the south. By means of this plan Warren was able, on a closely restricted lot, to provide the six flats on each floor with east, south, and west exposure. The general exterior treatment depended on a composition of simple elements—high rectangular openings, uninterrupted wall planes, slablike, sharp-edged volumes—for its architectonic effect. Warren introduced the horizontal courses above the third story to offset the pronounced upward movement resulting from the vertically elongated windows. A

1. *Industrial Chicago*, I, 243.

97. MONTGOMERY WARD WAREHOUSE, 1906–8

Detail of the river elevation. (*Commercial Photographic Co.*)

SCHMIDT, GARDEN AND MARTIN

98. DWIGHT BUILDING, 1911 SCHMIDT, GARDEN AND MARTIN

626 South Clark Street. (*Commercial Photographic Co.*)

99. HUNTER BUILDING, 1908 C. A. ECKSTROM

Now the Liberty Mutual Building, at 337 West Madison Street. The base was remodeled in 1948, then mostly cut off when the street level was raised in 1951 for the Wacker Drive extension. (*Chicago Architectural Photographing Co.*)

100. CHICAGO BUSINESS COLLEGE, 1910 — D. H. BURNHAM AND COMPANY

Now the Adams and Wabash Building, at the southeast corner of the intersection from which it takes its name. The Adams and Wabash is at the left side of the picture; the Hoops Building (taller than its neighbors) appears in the middle background, the Auditorium tower in the distance. (*Commercial Photographic Co.*)

101. SOCIETY BRAND BUILDING, 1913 GRAHAM, BURNHAM AND COMPANY
416 South Franklin Street. (*Commercial Photographic Co.*)

102. LEMOYNE BUILDING, 1914 — MUNDIE, JENSEN AND MCCLURG

180 North Wabash Avenue. (*Kaufmann & Fabry.*)

103. CARL SCHURZ HIGH SCHOOL, 1910 — Dwight Perkins

Milwaukee Avenue and Addison Street. (*Chicago Board of Education.*)

104. CARL SCHURZ HIGH SCHOOL, 1910 DWIGHT PERKINS

Detail of the roof and main elevation. (*Chicago Board of Education.*)

105. CARSON PIRIE SCOTT ANNEX, 1927 HUBERT AND DANIEL BURNHAM, JR.

Northwest corner of Wabash Avenue and Monroe Street. (*Williams & Meyer.*)

106. CARSON PIRIE SCOTT ANNEX, WEST ADDITIONS, 1940, 1950

The three bays on the left were formerly a garage designed by Louis Kroman and built in 1940. The bay in the center was added in 1949–50 to merge the two buildings. The extension is perfectly in keeping with the original structure. (*Allen Lein.*)

107. PROJECT, TRIBUNE TOWER COMPETITION, 1922

WALTER GROPIUS AND ADOLF MEYER

One of the few good designs to be submitted, its immediate precedent was the Chicago work of the eighties and nineties. (*From "The Tribune Tower Competition."*)

108. ALUMNI MEMORIAL HALL, ILLINOIS INSTITUTE OF TECHNOLOGY, 1946

LUDWIG MIES VAN DER ROHE AND ASSOCIATES

The campus extends along State Street from Thirty-first to Thirty-fifth. The Memorial Hall is one unit of a complete campus plan developed by Professor Van der Rohe, who is chairman of the Institute's Department of Architecture. (*Hedrich-Blessing Studio.*)

striking feature of this severe but effective design is the extreme narrowness of the spandrels.

The flats were divided into living-room, dining-room, bedroom, library, kitchen, and bathroom. The major innovation in interior design was the introduction of movable (folding) partitions so that the living and dining areas could be opened with the library into a single continuous room. This open interior plan became an important feature of Wright's houses around 1900 and is now nearly universal in contemporary domestic architecture. Gas ranges were standard equipment in the kitchens of the Virginia. All kitchens connected directly with the service elevators. A reversal of the usual arrangement appeared in the location of the laundry rooms on the top floor and the main dining-room in the basement. Electric lighting and steam heat completed the catalogue of modern utilitarian facilities. The Virginia Hotel was one of the first and finest modern structures of its class.

The sharp-edged rectangularity of the Virginia gave way to cylindrical corners and projecting bay windows in Warren's next large commission. It was the Metropole Hotel, erected about 1891 at Michigan Avenue and Twenty-third Street, where it still stands (Fig. 78). The Metropole, like the Virginia, is a series of separate blocks divided by deeply indented courts open at one end. Although it is three stories lower than the Virginia, its greater area of plan makes it about equal in size. Interior arrangements and facilities are essentially the same as those of the older building. Exterior treatment is considerably different and more nearly typical of the work of Warren and his contemporaries in the same field of design. Between the first story and the seventh Warren disposed all his windows in the circular and trapezoidal projections of the wall. The flat, unopened areas of the wall are relatively narrow; thus the total window area is large. The projections give the impression of its being somewhat larger than it is.

The present Hotel Michigan, built in 1891–92, follows in general the exterior treatment of the Metropole (Fig. 79). The Michigan, originally called the Lexington Hotel, stands at the northeast corner of Michigan Avenue and Cermak Road, one block north of its forerunner. The interest in form correlation undoubtedly lies in part behind the similarity of the two structures. The projecting bays and pavilions of the Michigan are narrower and shallower than those of the older building and stop three stories short of the parapet. The whole formal design is consequently less unified and less well integrated than that of the Metropole. It is a much larger structure and is a hotel rather than an apartment building.[2] It contains three hundred and seventy rooms arranged around an interior court. A steel frame carries the brick facing and ornamental terra-cotta trim.

The Plaza Hotel, erected in 1892 at 1553 North Clark Street, follows closely the plan, form, and general functional arrangement of the Metropole (Fig. 80). The whole structure is divided into three equal blocks separated by narrow courts extending through the depth of the building. The cylindrical extensions of the corners are repeated six times along the length of the façade, forming the dominant characteristic of the over-all pattern. The uniformity, regularity, and coherence of this design make it one of Warren's best. Like the Metropole and the Michigan, the Plaza has deteriorated badly, a result of urban blight which has spread out from the central area with the haphazard location of industries and warehouses and the growth of slums.

Warren's largest and best-executed commission was that for the Congress Hotel, which stands in sound state and full use today (Fig. 81). It is the finest architectural work among the leading downtown hotels in Chicago or, for that matter, in nearly any other city. The first or north block of the Congress, at 504 South Michigan Avenue (at Congress Street), was completed in 1893. The addition to the south was constructed in two parts: the first four bays in 1902, the remainder in 1907. Holabird and Roche received the commission for the annex but followed Warren's design exactly except for the treatment of the fenestration at the top four stories. Warren's handling of the original portion indicates a deliberate attempt to harmonize it with the Auditorium on the north corner of Congress Street.

2. The Chicago architects and builders used the terms indiscriminately.

The greater uniformity of Holabird's exterior design better expresses the steel-framed building than does Warren's. The four upper stories of the north block suggest its architect's handling of the Dexter Building as well as Sullivan's treatment of the Auditorium. As a whole, however, the Congress is a direct, simple, well-integrated work of structural art. In spite of the verticalism and the wide separation of the openings, the numerous projecting bay windows give the wall a rich texture and a light, glittering quality that well suggests the thin curtain drawn over the members of the interior frame. The architects of the Congress took full advantage of the most recent developments in structural and utilitarian elements. From the caisson foundations of the south block to the disposition of light switches in the rooms, the Congress was in every respect the herald of a new architectural period.

VARIATIONS ON THE STANDARD FORM

Many Chicago architects whose names are not associated with the development of the modern office building contributed important designs in the field of the multiple dwelling. One of the largest of the combined transient-residential hotels was the original Chicago Beach Hotel, at Hyde Park Boulevard and Cornell Street. It was first constructed about 1890, then rebuilt in 1911. The appearance and functional arrangements were so much like those of the Hyde Park Hotel that it was probably the work of the same builders, Starrett and Fuller. Frederick Baumann and J. K. Cady designed an exceptionally fine structure at Roosevelt Road and Michigan Avenue—the Bordeaux Apartments, erected in 1891. The closely grouped windows in projecting bays, characteristic of Warren's work, appeared here in a precise and severe composition of horizontal and vertical lines. Flanders and Zimmerman applied the principle of their Mallers Warehouse to the Park Gate Hotel, 1891–92, on Fifty-ninth Street. They opened the wall into an unusual area of glass extending over the flat surfaces and the projecting bays. The Park Gate was only six stories high but nearly a block long. Edmund R. Krause followed some of Warren's principles in his design of the Alexandria Hotel, erected in 1891 at 542 North Rush Street, where it still stands. One of the handsomest products of the movement initiated by Starrett and Warren is the Mecca Apartments, built in 1891–92 at the northwest corner of State and Thirty-fourth streets after the plans of Edbrooke and Burnham. The structure still stands, now sadly decayed. The Mecca is exceptionally fine by virtue of its smooth plane surfaces and precise modeling, emphasized by Roman brick. Each wing of the building has an interior light court roofed with glass and surrounded by continuous balconies, much like that of the Chamber of Commerce Building.

The high standard of design established by Starrett and Warren persisted up to the depression of 1893. When construction was resumed again, the boldness of spirit and fertility of imagination exhibited by the hotel architects began to give way before the fashionable classicism of the Fair. But many fine buildings were completed before the failure of business followed by the failure of nerve killed the spirit of the Chicago architects. The Omaha Apartments, designed by Irving K. and Allen B. Pond, were erected in 1893. Although the window area was relatively small, covering less than half of the main elevation, the openings were distributed over the usual projecting bays. The over-all treatment was crisp and precise, befitting the architecture of an age of industry and technology. The ornament of the Omaha was reduced to an unobtrusive trim at base and cornice, the architectonic effect growing out of extensive planes and sharply incised openings. The Lakota Hotel, 1893, at the southeast corner of Michigan Avenue and Thirtieth Street, was typical of the hotel as it was developed by Starrett and Warren (Fig. 82).[3] The corner pavilions, the bay windows, the grouped openings, the deep, narrow court, the uniformity and regularity of the elevations—these together with its functional interior design make it one of the good late examples of its class.

The Brewster Apartments, built about 1893 at the corner of Diversey Parkway and Pine Grove Avenue, is an unusual varia-

3. I have been unable to discover the name of the architect. The Lakota may have been done by Warren, but the little domes and the smooth, heavy stonework of the base suggest another hand.

tion on the standard form (Fig. 83). The Brewster was designed by R. H. Turnock, a product of William Le Baron Jenney's office. In the treatment of openings and projections in the wall it belongs to the main stream of hotel architecture. What distinguishes it from the rest of its kind is its massive envelope of rough-cut stone. Turnock may have been influenced in this respect by Richardson, who was very fond of the romantic effect produced by this rich and heavy texture. The plan of the Brewster is a hollow rectangle around a central court. In order to admit as much light to the lobby as possible, Turnock used treads of plate glass in the main stairway, thus allowing light to filter through the entire eight stories from the roof skylight to the lobby on the main floor.

The original architecture of hotels and apartments survived in isolated buildings during the late nineties. Except for the last addition to the Congress Hotel (1907), the Langdon Apartments on Des Plaines Avenue were the final product of the new Chicago movement. The Langdon was designed by Dwight Perkins and constructed in 1903. The bay windows, the large openings, and the simple, straightforward treatment, with its emphasis on volume and plane, distinguish this structure from the vulgarity growing up around it. Yet the sound principles of design developed in the late eighties never wholly disappeared. They survived in scores of anonymous apartment buildings constructed as late as 1929 and often designed by the contractors who built them. They appear on the North Side, in Hyde Park, Rogers Park, and Evanston, and in some of the other outlying towns. One may distinguish them by their simplicity and honesty of appearance, their freedom from redundant and derivative ornament, their large grouped windows, and, in many cases, their deep glass-inclosed projections, square in plan, providing solariums or living-rooms with three-way exposure. They form part of the precarious but vital continuity which joins the Chicago school to the world-wide movement of the new architecture.

CHAPTER XI

The Chicago School in the Twentieth Century

WE HAVE traced the development of the new architectural movement in Chicago up to 1900. The melancholy collapse of the movement at the end of the nineties is well known, and its causes have been investigated. When building activity was resumed after the depression of 1893, the Chicago architects for the most part turned away from the original and organic style which they had developed. They bowed in abject humility before the learned imitators of the East—Hunt, McKim, Carrère, Hastings, and others. They did not know that emancipated spirits in Europe were finding independent solutions similar to their own. They forgot about Frank Lloyd Wright and the little handful of men led by Richard Schmidt who tried to keep architecture alive. Many of them died around the turn of the century, and their followers devoted what talent they had to creating the architectural zoos of Wacker Drive and North Michigan Avenue. What the structural art became, however, was what the clients wanted. We deserve the buildings that we get.

After the Civil War the industrialists and capitalists of the Chicago area rightly thought of themselves as financiers and organizers, makers of industries and railroads. They felt at home in the bold and vigorous work of the Chicago school. By 1900, however, they had created a new imperialism and began to think of themselves as an aristocracy of wealth and breeding. In imitation of their fellows in the East, they wanted a setting which would reflect historical precedent, honorable traditions, and baronial power. This change followed an alteration in the economy of Chicago. The men who made Chicago were builders, inventors, and manufacturers. Their counterparts in the East were financial operators and manipulators. But by 1900 the industrialists and manufacturers of Chicago, their position consolidated, became the manipulators of banks and exchanges. The city remained a center of manufacture and transportation, but its control passed to men whose power was symbolized by the Wheat Pit rather than by the mills and factories of the harbor belt. Money is not real wealth, and an architecture of money may easily become an unreal thing—especially when philistinism and materialism characterize those who commission it.

But the vigor and essential soundness of the Chicago movement could not be easily destroyed. Its basic principles and its incomparable mastery of the structural art survived in isolated men and buildings well into the twentieth century. Holabird and Roche continued to design fine buildings equal to the high standard of their previous work. It is significant, however, that the best of it stood outside the commercial area of the Loop. Sullivan's last great building marked the high point of the Chicago school. Dwight Perkins, Richard Schmidt, and a handful of lesser figures tried with some success to maintain the principles of Root and Jenney and Warren. A few European architects, notably Walter Gropius, developed an architecture which was in part a direct outgrowth of the innovations made by the Chicago architects. By the 1920's, however, architecture in Chicago was most perfectly symbolized by the Tribune Tower; thirty years before, it was the second Leiter Building.

THE CARSON PIRIE SCOTT STORE

Sullivan's career in the twentieth century was a record of neglect and poverty. A defiant and bitter rebel, he refused to compromise with the conspicuous extravagance of the new eclecticism. His inflexible and arrogant personality made it difficult even for sympathetic clients to deal with him. He was a severe disciplinarian in his office, and he carried his extremely high standards into his business dealings. The result was that he was always admired and feared but rarely liked. He poured out his scorn for the World's Fair, the classicism of the East, Burnham the impresario, the Tribune Tower, and everything these phenomena represented in his *Autobiography of an Idea*, in the *Kindergarten Chats*, and in numerous articles and letters. He became a crusader and a pamphleteer, turning the vision of a great creative artist into the only medium of expression left him. In his later life he was indeed a prophet without honor. He was often praised in Europe, where many architects and critics who regarded him as the greatest architect in the United States were astonished at his lack of commissions.

It is fortunate for architecture everywhere that Sullivan enjoyed one more opportunity to design a large urban building. The commission for the Carson Pirie Scott Store was his last chance to express his powers on the scale and in the milieu to which the Chicago architects were accustomed. In the full vigor of his middle age, as yet free of the bitter contempt of his last years, he put into it everything that he had as a thinker, an artist, and an engineer. The building is known and admired today wherever an interest in architecture flourishes.

The old firm of Schlesinger and Mayer, owners of a dry-goods business since Civil War days, engaged Adler and Sullivan in 1891 to design an addition to their original building at State and Madison streets, constructed in 1873 after the plans of W. W. Boyington, and to bring the original and the addition together behind a uniform façade. The depression of 1893 stopped the project, which languished for six years. Meanwhile Adler and Sullivan had separated. In 1899 the firm decided to build an entirely new building along Madison Street as a separate unit from the old building which stood at the southeast corner of State and Madison and extended a short distance south along State. They selected Sullivan, rather than Adler, as the architect. The new 1899 structure, which Sullivan designed, was three bays wide and nine stories high and stood at Madison Street somewhat east of the intersection with State. It constituted the first portion of the present Carson Pirie Scott Store. In 1902 the old buildings at the corner were demolished, and in the following year Sullivan designed the extension of the Madison Street store. This addition, twelve stories high, consisting of three bays along Madison and seven along State, was built in 1903–4. In the latter year Carson Pirie Scott and Company bought the business from Schlesinger and Mayer. In 1906 D. H. Burnham and Company were commissioned to design the last addition, the five south bays on State Street, which were constructed in the same year. Burnham wisely elected to follow Sullivan's plans in every detail except in the treatment of the top story. Thus the completed building—six bays on Madison and twelve on State—emerged in steps (Fig. 84). It remained unchanged until 1948, when the original cornice or roof projection was replaced by a parapet (Fig. 85).

The Carson Pirie Scott Store is a completely steel-framed structure the skeleton of which rests on a caisson foundation extending to bedrock. The outer columns and spandrel beams above the second story are sheathed in thin tiles of terra cotta. The first two stories, constituting the base, are clothed in cast iron covered with a remarkably profuse, delicate, and original foliate ornament of low relief—the personal stamp of the architect's highly individualistic genius. A narrow band of this ornament appears along the bottom of the detail illustration (Fig. 86). The elaborate pattern of intertwining leaflike forms was sketched in general form by Sullivan, worked out in detail by George Grant Elmslie, a member of Sullivan's office for several years following the dissolution of the partnership, and executed in plaster molds by Kristian Schneider, a sculptor who had handled Sullivan's ornament for twenty years.

There has been much discussion of the intrinsic aesthetic quality of the lavish ornament at the base of the Carson Pirie Scott Store. However one may feel about it as a pattern, it is nevertheless true that its lyric and romantic quality is not appropriate to the kind of expression which the store represents. But we can say in Sullivan's defense that he kept it flat and properly subordinated to the main elements of the form, on which the architectural effect of the building depends.

Above the ornamental base rise the great cellular elevations, bold and exact and perfectly proportioned articulations of the steel frame. An overhanging roof slab or cornice originally terminated the structure, a much more satisfactory element than the present parapet, which is badly out of scale with the spandrels (Fig. 85). The transition between the street elevations is effected by means of a cylindrical pavilion at the corner, where the main entrance is located. The natural horizontality of the Chicago windows is deliberately emphasized by the ornamental bands extending continuously along the sill and lintel lines (Fig. 86). Aside from these bands, the elevations above the base have a cleanliness and precision so nearly absolute that the most minute change in proportions could be immediately detected. There is no better revelation of the architecture of mechanized industrialism.

The flow of space on the interior of the Carson Pirie Scott Store has been dammed and parceled by the many partitions forming the separate inclosures common to large department stores. The building is a closed rectangle of straight warehouse construction. The interior, consequently, appears as a series of broad avenues separated by the slender, widely spaced columns. It rises with complete uniformity through one floor after another, except that the ceiling height of the three top stories is smaller than that of the first nine stories (the reduction appears clearly in the illustrations: Figs. 84 and 85).

The department store of Carson Pirie Scott and Company is Sullivan's swan song and his unchallenged masterpiece. It is the ultimate achievement of the Chicago school and one of the great works of modern commercial architecture in the world. Both the system of construction and its formal expression evolved directly out of the work of Jenney and Holabird. What distinguishes it from the best of their designs are the thoroughness of Sullivan's exploitation of aesthetic possibilities and his superior sense of scale, proportion, regularity, and organization. The elevations present a powerful and dynamic revelation of the steel cage that carries the building: thrust and counterthrust, the forces of tension and compression, are actually felt by the observer. The huge west façade is a repetitive pattern of rectangular cells, skilfully carried around the corner to the north wall by means of the pavilion which repeats on smaller scale and in subtle variation the motive of the walls. To the forceful statement of structure, deep reveals add clarity and incisiveness. The logic and precision of science and technology are translated into an aesthetic discipline of grace and dignity born out of exact and controlled strength. Formal, structural, and utilitarian elements are fully integrated into a new and prophetic synthesis.

After the Carson store Sullivan's commissions dwindled away into a handful of little banks and suburban stores. There were two more in Chicago: the first was the Felsenthal Store, 701 East Forty-seventh Street, 1905; the second, the last commission of his life, was the Krause Music Store, 4611 Lincoln Avenue, 1922. The Felsenthal building represents the pure personal idiom and points toward the "expressionism" of the country banks done between 1907 and 1919. Large areas of unbroken wall surface emphasize mass and solidity while at the same time suggesting the compositions of basic geometric forms characterizing the banks and a great deal of modern architecture.

Sullivan's work is surprisingly uneven for so great a man. Yet whatever he touched came alive, and he could rise to such heights of aesthetic and moral power that even his detractors approached him in humility. Few men have the courage of conviction he showed in his last years, but men of spirit everywhere are thankful that he had it.

THE LATE WORK OF HOLABIRD AND ROCHE

The basic type of commercial block which Holabird and Roche perfected continued to appear in a number of good designs during the first decade of the new century. The cellular elevations, continuous piers, wide Chicago windows, or grouped windows of standard size reveal themselves in clean-cut lines and careful proportions. They have been described at length before and need no extended comment here. The important commissions of Holabird and Roche which show little variation on the fundamental theme are the following: the original Powers Building, now known as the Champlain, northeast corner of Monroe Street and Wabash Avenue, 1903 (Fig. 87); the two north bays of the Bailey Building, 529 South Franklin Street, 1898, of which the three south bays, erected in 1903, were designed by Nimmons and Fellows (Fig. 88); the 325 West Jackson Building, 1904, 1911, the finest of all in its exact regularity and harmony (Fig. 89); and the Born Building, 540 South Wells Street, 1908 (Fig. 90). An addition to the Born Building, designed by A. S. Alschuler, was constructed in 1927.

Of these structures, the Champlain is worth further consideration because of the alteration of the base made a few years ago. Several bays of the first two stories at the corner were remodeled in 1946 for the ticket office of the Trans World Airline, the design of which was the work of Skidmore, Owings and Merrill. This handsome and sophisticated work of contemporary architecture involved the dissolution of the wall at the base into a continuous area of glass. The result is that modernization in this case is entirely in keeping with the over-all form and expression of the building. The best way to modernize the structures of the Chicago school is to do what its own architects did, that is, to clothe the base in glass. The common use of a shiny synthetic material as an envelope for many contemporary store fronts has ruined the base of a number of fine Chicago buildings.

Holabird and Roche returned to the projecting bay windows of the Tacoma in the Chicago Building, erected in 1904 at the southwest corner of State and Madison streets (Fig. 91). In this structure, however, a modification of the Chicago window takes the place of the narrow sash in the older building. The wide windows of the Chicago almost fill the alternate flat and projecting bays along the Madison Street elevation, with the result that the walls are dissolved into a glittering pattern of light reflected from several angles. The unification of this diversity of elements is well handled from the standpoint of proportion, but an ambiguity appears in the sharp verticalism of the projecting bays set off against the horizontality of the main wall plane. The rustication of the corners recalls the Marquette Building.

Further variations on the uninterrupted cellular wall appear in three late structures. The nineteen-story Republic Building is one of the cleanest and sharpest of all Holabird and Roche's designs, a result partly of the long and very tenuous piers (Fig. 92). The Republic stands at 209 South State Street. It was originally opened in 1905, but additional stories were constructed in 1909. The annex of Mandel Brothers Store, built in 1906 at the northwest corner of Wabash Avenue and Madison Street, is unusual for its great horizontal elongation, the product of very wide bays and narrow spandrels (Fig. 93). Another striking feature is the continuous opening of the second story, a small portion of which appears in the lower right-hand corner of the illustration. The Brooks Building, erected in 1909–10 at 223 West Jackson Boulevard, concluded the original work of Holabird and Roche (Fig. 94). It is one of the best unified and most open of their designs. The sense of lightness and sharpness conveyed by the elevations is partly a consequence of the concentric round moldings on the piers, which elongate and narrow their appearance. Holabird and Roche were fortunate in the preservation of their buildings: almost all of their good designs after the Tacoma stand today.[1]

THE WORK OF RICHARD E. SCHMIDT

The classical debauch and other varieties of historical eclecticism which followed the World's Fair did not, as we have seen, go unchallenged. Some of the older architects continued to do excellent work after the upturn of economic activity in 1897. What is more significant is the fact that the Chicago school, in the day of its decline, had begun to influence a number of younger men who were determined to keep alive its principles in their own work. The leader among them was Frank Lloyd Wright, who had been trained in Sullivan's office and who has always referred to him as "Lieber Meister." The others were Richard E. Schmidt, Irving K. Pond, Hugh Garden, George Maher, George Dean, Robert Spencer, and Howard Shaw. These earnest and forward-looking young men met at intervals during the nineties to discuss and criticize each other's work

1. The essential form of the original work of Holabird and Roche persists in the Great Lakes Building, Wacker Drive, 1912, and the Crane Building, Michigan Avenue, 1913, but thereafter it disappears entirely.

and to devise means of combating the fashionable eclecticism of the time. For the most part they followed Wright into residential design, but a few of them enjoyed commissions for larger buildings. Pond designed several apartments, and Maher drew the plans for the original Patten Gymnasium at Northwestern University. Much of their work suffered, however, from an excessive dependence on personal idiom and a failure to understand the organic structuralism of the Chicago movement. In the field of commercial and industrial architecture Richard Schmidt and his partner Hugh Garden—both of whom are alive today—were clearly superior to all of them.

The best work of the firm Schmidt, Garden and Martin appeared around 1910. Their designs are good in exact proportion to the consistency with which they pursued the aims of the Chicago school. Schmidt was the leader and chief designing talent of the firm, and it was his ability as a creative architect that lies behind the distinguishing features of their buildings. He was born at Ebern, Bavaria, in 1865 and came to the United States in 1883. He attended Massachusetts Institute of Technology for two years (1883–85), but he decided to start his career as an architect before completing the curriculum. He began individual practice in Chicago in 1887. The partnership of Schmidt, Garden and Martin was established in 1906. Richard Schmidt's attitude toward design was not uniform, varying from the expression of a personal idiom to the impersonal revelation of the structure and function of a building. If there was a particular influence in his work, it was that of Sullivan or Wright rather than Holabird or Jenney or Root.

The ambiguity which may result when a functional and organic form is in part sacrificed to a personal feeling for pure abstract form appears in Schmidt's Nepeenauk (formerly Chapin and Gore) Building, built in 1901–2 at 63 East Adams Street (Fig. 95). The façade is the product of a plastic handling of the major elements composing it. Above the third story the wall appears to start from the formal expression of steel framing, yet the unusually deep reveals, the massive piers, and the heavy spandrel at the top suggest masonry construction which has been molded to reflect the sharp edges, plane surfaces, and obvious organization appropriate to machine products or to the machine itself. The capricious introduction of a separate and totally inorganic treatment of the wall at the second and third stories is the outgrowth of pure personal feeling. Schmidt had developed a similar but more refined expression of the timber framing of the Grommes and Ullrich Warehouse, 111 West Illinois Street, erected in 1901.

The same fondness for playing with surfaces in an emotional rather than an organic way lies behind the outer form of the powerhouse of the Schoenhofen Brewery, erected in 1902 at Eighteenth Street and Canalport Avenue. The elevations are sharp-edged rectangular planes which in profile and texture exactly express the nature of the brick curtain wall. But the openings are grouped in arbitrary vertical bands separated by false piers with recessed spandrels between them (the skyscraper accent of the Wainwright and Prudential buildings). The vertical lines are grouped in turn into five panels along the main or southeast elevation, thus further denying the nature and the unity of the structural system employed. But the Schoenhofen powerhouse was so far in advance of the shallow copybook architecture growing up everywhere that Russell Sturgis singled it out for special discussion as a work of genuine and original structural art, something which could never come out of the schools. "No school of architecture," he wrote, "can teach a man how to design such buildings as this brewery. At least, if there be any school of architecture of that stamp, it should really proclaim itself—its power of inspiring liberal and practical ideas in the youthful mind should be widely advertised. As things are, we dread the going of a student to an architectural school, and we dread accepting him as an assistant when he leaves that school; and this because of the perfunctory nature of what he learns there. No blame to anyone! He would be a bold professor of architecture who would try and lead his boys to the designing of things according to the requirements of the situation."[2]

2. "The Schoenhofen Brewery," *Architectural Record*, XVII (March, 1905), 201.

The building designed by Schmidt, Garden and Martin which indubitably stands by itself as a great work of architecture is the warehouse of Montgomery Ward and Company, extending along the North Branch of the Chicago River at West Chicago Avenue (Fig. 96). It was Schmidt's most important commission after Michael Reese Hospital, completed in 1906. The warehouse, a tremendous structure, was built over a period of nearly three years, from 1906 to 1908. Here the plastic handling of form characteristic of Sullivan or Wright is properly subordinated to and informed by the structural and functional nature of the building. The Montgomery Ward warehouse is eight stories high (nine along the river), 800 feet long, with an average width of nearly 200 feet, and 158,000 square feet in area of plan. This immense volume was treated with an honesty, sureness, and directness worthy of the best architects of the Chicago school. The elevations take their form from the system of construction, but they are at the same time revelations of a pure artistic idea intuitively related to the fundamental aims of the school and of the general movement in the graphic and structural arts of the time.

The Montgomery Ward warehouse was the first building of the school to be supported by a reinforced concrete frame. The heavy columns and beams of the skeleton are directly reflected in the pattern of horizontal and vertical bands which forms the dominant accent of the elevations. As a matter of fact, with the exception of the brick facing on the spandrels, the elevations are composed of the outer members of the frame itself. On this direct revelation of structure Schmidt imposed a strong horizontality achieved by means of narrow projecting bands at the top and bottom of each spandrel (Fig. 97). It is the horizontality of Sullivan's Meyer Building, but here a more logical product of the form dictated by the material of the frame as well as a recognition of the natural horizontality of the multistory building. The sweeping horizontal planes and long bands of Wright's Robie house, also completed in 1908, represent something of the same aesthetic intuition.

The three-story factory of the Garden City Plating and Manufacturing Company, at Tallmadge and Ogden avenues, pointed toward the most effective of Schmidt's designs. This structure, erected in 1910, had the articulated cellular wall of the Carson Pirie Scott Store, but excessively wide piers and spandrels detracted from its possible sharpness and clarity. The Garden City factory was the preliminary step to the incisive, open, finely proportioned façade of the Dwight Building, at 626 South Clark Street, constructed in 1911 (Fig. 98). The treatment of the main elevation recalls the Nepeenauk, but the narrow piers and spandrels, the horizontal emphasis of the wide windows, the shallow reveals, and the uniformity of the composition make the Dwight far superior to the earlier structure. The Dwight Building is certainly equal to the best work of Holabird and Roche, superior, perhaps, in the absence of the heavy cornice and stout corner piers so common in their work.

ISOLATED ACHIEVEMENTS

From time to time up to the first World War good buildings were constructed which embodied the high standards of the Chicago school. They were usually designed by architects the bulk of whose work was of transitory interest, but who, in one structure or another, showed that they possessed a little of the old emancipation and vigor of the eighties and nineties. The precedent for most of them was the articulated wall of Jenney's Sears Roebuck Store, as it was refined by Holabird and Roche. The original Hunter Building, designed by C. A. Eckstrom, is the best of the isolated achievements (Fig. 99). Now the office building of the Liberty Mutual Insurance Company, it was constructed in 1908 at 337 West Madison Street. The stores at the base were removed prior to the remodeling of the ground floor in 1947–48. This alteration resulted in considerable improvement, the first story having been opened into a succession of large glass areas each filling the entire bay with an uninterrupted pane. In its purity and regularity the Liberty Mutual Building stands with the clearest expressions of the architecture of steel framing.

The old Chicago Business College, now the Adams and Wabash Building, is a late variation on the same principle (Fig. 100). The narrowness of the piers compared to the width of the spandrels, together with the unusually wide Chicago windows, produces an exaggerated horizontality. The building, on the southeast corner of the intersection from which it takes its name, was erected in 1910 after the plans of D. H. Burnham and Company. The adaptation of the Chicago office building to industrial purposes was a logical consequence of opening the wall to the maximum extent allowable with wide-bayed steel framing. Many industrial and manufacturing structures were built in the area around the Loop from 1900 to 1925, and a considerable proportion of them exhibit the same basic form as does the Sears Roebuck Store. One of the best is Graham, Burnham and Company's Society Brand Building, at 416 South Franklin Street, erected in 1913 (Fig. 101). It is certainly better in its clarity and openness than the same firm's comparable but more famous Butler Brothers Warehouse, 1913, at Canal and Lake streets, and Marshall Field Store, 1902, 1914, on State Street between Randolph and Washington. One of the last structures in the Loop to represent the moribund Chicago school is the Lemoyne Building, originally a combination of hotel, offices, and stores but now simply an office block (Fig. 102). It was erected in 1914 at 180 North Wabash Avenue, after the plans of Mundie, Jensen and McClurg, inheritors of Jenney's business.

CARL SCHURZ HIGH SCHOOL

The only public building which can properly be classed with the work of the Chicago school represents the line of development of Sullivan, Wright, and Schmidt rather than of Jenney and Holabird. It is Carl Schurz High School, at Milwaukee Avenue and Addison Street, built in 1910 (Figs. 103 and 104). Dwight Perkins, who had come from Burnham's office, was the architect. The school is an impressive example of personal and formal expression on a large scale. In plan it consists of a central east-west portion from which two long wings spread out on diagonal lines, the whole structure nearly a block long in overall length. The building is dominated by a huge steeply pitched roof of green tile, almost overpowering in immediate effect. It is a thoroughly functional design except for the interior corridors, which receive no natural light. The spreading plan and the location, well back from the streets on spacious lawns, represent a happy solution to the problem of orientation for light and air and reasonable freedom from the noise of traffic.

The exterior treatment of Carl Schurz is not organic so far as its structure is concerned. Again it represents a case of treating the total form of a building as a plastic thing to be molded according to the feeling of the architect. Pure forms, sharp-edged intersections, uninterrupted planes, a dominating horizontal line—some of the marks of Wright's personal idiom—give the school its important place in the anonymous and constituent aims of the period. The emphasis of the wall is sharply vertical, secured by introducing closely spaced false piers into the elevation. This accent is uniform throughout the length of all elevations. The verticalism, however, is abruptly terminated and effectively controlled by the stone course at the top of the heavy pylons at the corners and flanking the entranceway. It is a formal element characteristic of a number of Wright's early designs, such as Unity Church, Hillside School, the Larkin Company administration building, and many residences of the period around 1910. A part of the effectiveness of Carl Schurz High School lies in its color: the brick envelope of the wall is burnt red, the roof green, the stone trim light buff. Although the school lies outside the main stream of Chicago work, it is a brilliant exhibition of virtuosity comparable to Wright's prairie houses and Sullivan's banks. It belongs to the architecture which has evolved out of our attempts—often romantic—to develop an organic assimilation of the techniques of a mechanized culture.

THE CARSON PIRIE SCOTT ANNEX

Many years after the Chicago school succumbed to the new eclecticism of the twentieth century, shortly before both European and American architecture became related parts of the world-wide progress of the new movement, another structure took its place beside the original work of the eighties and nineties. It is the largest building of the group comprising the Carson Pirie Scott Annex or Men's Store, located at the northwest corner of Wabash Avenue and Monroe Street (Fig. 105). This building was constructed in 1927 after the plans of Hubert and Daniel Burnham, Jr. The entire annex has now expanded into two other buildings flanking it. On the north, along Wabash, is the old Thomas Church Building, designed by Hill and Woltersdorf and constructed in 1903 (four more stories were added in 1949–50). On the west, along Monroe, is a former garage erected in 1940 after the plans of Louis Kroman. The façade of this structure grows directly out of the cellular wall of the early Chicago work. The remodeling of the garage and the addition of a single bay to merge it with the store building were completed in 1950. The merging of the separate structures presents a nearly uniform and continuous façade along the north side of Monroe Street (Fig. 106). Thus two-thirds of the block from Wabash to State is dominated by as impressive a work of commercial architecture as the Chicago movement produced.

The construction and essential form of the Carson Pirie Scott Annex are no different from those of many other buildings we have described. The precedent was plainly the main store designed by Louis Sullivan at State and Madison. It remains simply to point out the level of sophistication and urbanity which the Burnham Brothers achieved in this building. Except for the narrow bands of ornamental terra cotta at the sill and lintel lines of each story and the scarcely noticeable classical garland at the parapet, the architects depended upon the perfect articulation of the steel frame for their architectonic effect. Although the proportions and over-all dimensions are different from those of the main store, the Annex building impresses one with the same sense of power and clarity and grace. Indeed, it is superior to Sullivan's building in one respect: by treating the base in much the same way that they handled the elevations above it, the architects of the Annex secured a better-integrated composition. They differentiated the first two stories only by setting the windows flush with the outer faces of piers and spandrels instead of placing them in deep reveals, as in the stories above. The finest works of commercial architecture erected after the second World War reveal no higher sense of order and unity than this building can show.

THE INFLUENCE OF THE CHICAGO SCHOOL

Frank Lloyd Wright, more than anyone else, maintained the continuity that joins Sullivan to the architecture of our own day. But Wright's debt to the older man was a formal and aesthetic one translated into unique and personal terms. The Chicago school achieved its greatness in the more anonymous and impersonal terms of commercial architecture—office buildings and hotels—and it is in this field that we ought to look for influence in the further evolution of the structural art.

Actually the school had no direct influence on the immediate development of commercial architecture after 1900. With rare exceptions the whole course of that development lay in the opposite direction. By 1910 the work of Sullivan, Jenney, Root, and even Wright seemed old-fashioned and crude. The successful architects, including some who had achieved distinction in the Chicago school, deliberately turned their backs on the movement that created the Leiter buildings and the Carson Pirie Scott Store. The result of this retreat into sham architecture is apparent in every city. It forms the very picture of confusion. It is ironic but instructive that some of the worst products should have appeared in Chicago—the classical style of Union Station, the Gothic of the Tribune Tower, the Baroque of the Pure Oil Building.

As Russell Sturgis pointed out, however, one had to look for progress toward a genuine structural art in what he called "non-architectural" buildings, like the powerhouse of the Schoenhofen Brewery. The industrial architects, independent of the Chicago school and somewhat after the time it flourished, created a significant architecture by arriving at the same solutions achieved by the Chicago group. Albert Kahn's Brown-Lipe-Chapin factory in Syracuse (1908) and the Pittsburgh and Lake Erie warehouse in Pittsburgh (1917) are first-rate examples of the new industrial architecture that grew out of the same principles which produced Jenney's Sears Roebuck Store. And it was industrial building that grew to have one of the strongest influences on the new movement which became world wide by 1930. Kahn began his career in Chicago (Sullivan once offered him a job as a draftsman) and probably drew his major inspiration from the work of the Chicago school. He later became the country's greatest industrial architect

In Europe around 1910 an organic structural art began to emerge, chiefly in the work of Auguste Perret and Peter Behrens. The methods of construction and formal expression which they developed were essentially like those of the Chicago school. But there was no direct connection between the two groups, as there was between Wright and the Dutch architects after 1910. Yet the new work in Europe and in Chicago converged at one point in the next decade. Walter Gropius, who had studied under Behrens, and his associate Adolf Meyer submitted a project for the Tribune Tower competition of 1922 (Fig. 107). Their entry was one of the few of genuine merit to be submitted. The rest of them, taken together, marked the low point of the structural art in the past century and a half. The starting point for Grophius and Meyer's design was the newsprint warehouse, which still stands behind the present Tribune Tower along the river. The warehouse is typical of the commercial architecture developed by the Chicago school. Gropius and Meyer narrowed the piers and spandrels, employed the Chicago window in the openings, refined away redundant details, and produced one of the most sophisticated skyscraper designs of our time. It still remains to be embodied in the steel and glass of building.

From architects like Gropius and Le Corbusier and Mies van der Rohe the new movement eventually came back to the United States. After hesitant adaptations and experiments in horizontality and verticality, the American architects finally rediscovered an organic structural art which represents a logical synthesis of the European work of the 1920's and the Chicago achievement of the eighties and nineties. Today the articulated wall, taking its architectonic power from the formal possibilities of framed construction, is the mark of much of the best recent American architecture. Or it may be the lively and inexhaustible qualities of glass, made available by the same structural technique, that bring us the new beauties of contemporary work.

It is perfectly fitting that the architecture of the Chicago school should receive its ultimate refinement in Chicago itself by one of the great European pioneers of the new movement, Ludwig Mies van der Rohe. His recent buildings at Illinois Institute of Technology form the contemporary statement of principles developed in Chicago as early as 1879. The Alumni Memorial Hall, built in 1946 as one unit in an extensive campus plan, is perhaps the best of those so far completed (Fig. 108). His Promontory Apartments, opened for occupancy in 1949, with its exposed continuous columns in the elevations, comes even closer to the original Chicago work. In the skyscraper towers of 860 Lake Shore Drive, under construction in 1950, he achieved the final dissolution of the wall into glass.

Much new work in the years since the second World War has contributed to the revival of Chicago's former architectural preeminence. Some of it is the product of large and well-established firms of architects—Ogden Courts of the Chicago Housing Authority, by Skidmore, Owings and Merrill; the new apartments at 1350 North Lake Shore Drive, by Loebl, Schlossman and Bennett; two apartment buildings in the 3000 block on Sheridan Road, the work of Shaw, Metz and Dolio; the Kling Studio on Ohio Street, designed by Henry P. Glas and Friedman, Alschuler and Sincere; schools and housing projects by Perkins and Will and George Fred Keck. New apartment buildings have lately offered the best opportunities to the architects, among whom certain younger men, or at least newcomers to Chicago, have done important work—Pace Associates, who have collaborated extensively with Mies van der Rohe, have ten exceptionally fine buildings already to their credit, while Monroe Bowman, Joseph Gutnayer, Homer Rissman, and Harry Weese are the designers of a number of sophisticated and urbane apartments constructed during the building revival that came about four years after the close of the war. It is all mature work, with the long precedent of the great structural art of Chicago behind it. The damage wrought by the World's Fair lasted for fifty years, but we appear to have survived it.

Bibliography

Adler, Dankmar. "The Chicago Auditorium," *Architectural Record*, I, No. 4 (April–June, 1892), 415.

———. "Foundation Construction, Auditorium Building, Chicago," *Inland Architect and News Record*, Vol. XI, No. 3 (April, 1888) (unpaged).

———. "Foundations," *Industrial Chicago*, I, 473–78. (Originally published in *Economist*, June 25, 1891.)

Andreas, A. T. *History of Chicago*. Chicago, 1885–86.

Behrendt, Walter C. *Modern Building*. New York, 1937.

Chicago and Its Resources Twenty Years After, 1871–1891. Chicago, 1892.

Condit, Carl W. "The Chicago School and the Modern Movement in Architecture," *Art in America*, XXXVI, No. 1 (January, 1948), 19–37.

Dictionary of American Biography. New York, 1936. Articles on William Le Baron Jenney and William Holabird.

Fireproof Building Construction: Prominent Buildings Erected by the George A. Fuller Company. New York and Chicago, 1904.

Flinn, John J. *The Standard Guide to Chicago*. Chicago, 1892.

Freitag, J. K. *Architectural Engineering, with Special Reference to High Building Construction*. 3d ed. New York, 1912.

Giedion, Sigfried. *Space, Time and Architecture*. Cambridge, Mass., 1941.

Gilbert, Paul, and Bryson, Charles Lee. *Chicago and Its Makers*. Chicago, 1929.

Holcombe, Paul. *Depreciation and Obsolescence in the Tacoma Building*. Chicago: National Association of Building Owners and Managers, 1929.

Industrial Chicago. Chicago, 1891.

Jenney, W. L. B. "The Chicago Construction, or Tall Buildings on a Compressible Soil," *Inland Architect and News Record*, Vol. XVIII, No. 4 (November, 1891) (unpaged).

———. "A Few Practical Hints," *Inland Architect and News Record*, XIII, No. 1, 7–9.

Jevne and Almini. *Chicago Illustrated* (a portfolio of rare prints in the possession of the Chicago Historical Society).

Mendelsohn, Felix. *Chicago—Yesterday and Today*. Chicago, 1932.

Monroe, Harriet. *John Wellborn Root*. New York and Boston, 1896.

Moore, Charles H. *Daniel Hudson Burnham, Architect, Planner of Cities*. New York and Boston, 1921.

Morrison, Hugh. *Louis Sullivan, Prophet of Modern Architecture*. New York, 1935.

MUMFORD, LEWIS. *The Brown Decades*. New York, 1931.

MUSEUM OF MODERN ART. *Early Modern Architecture in Chicago, 1870–1910*. New York, 1940.

OREAR, G. W. *Commercial and Architectural Chicago*. Chicago, 1887.

PECK, RALPH B. *History of Building Foundations in Chicago*. ("University of Illinois Bulletin," Vol. XLV, No. 29.) Urbana, 1948.

Prominent Buildings Erected by the George A. Fuller Company. Chicago, 1893.

RANDALL, FRANK A. *History of the Development of Building Construction in Chicago*. Urbana, 1949.

REBORI, A. N. "The Work of Burnham and Root," *Architectural Record*, XXXVIII, No. 1 (July, 1915), 33–168.

SCHUYLER, MONTGOMERY. "A Critique of the Works of Adler and Sullivan," *Architectural Record*. December, 1895. ("Great American Architects Series," No. 2.)

SULLIVAN, LOUIS. *The Autobiography of an Idea*. New York, 1926.

———. *Kindergarten Chats*. New York, 1947.

TALLMADGE, THOMAS E. *Architecture in Old Chicago*. Chicago, 1941.

UPJOHN, E. M. "Buffington and the Skyscraper," *Art Bulletin*, XVII (March, 1935), 48–70.

WOLTERSDORF, ARTHUR. "Dankmar Adler," *Western Architect*, XXXIII, No. 7 (July, 1924), 75.

In addition, the following periodicals were consulted: *American Architecture*, *Architectural Record*, *Architectural Review*, *Architecture*, *Brickbuilder*, *Engineering News*, *Engineering Record*, *Inland Architect*, *Inland Architect and News Record*, *Land Owner*, and *Western Architect*.

Index

[Buildings known only by street numbers appear at the end of the Index.]

PRINTED IN U·S·A·